T0328706

Cambridge Elements

Elements in Islam and the Sciences
edited by
Nidhal Guessoum
American University of Sharjah, United Arab Emirates
Stefano Bigliardi
Al Akhawayn University in Ifrane, Morocco

ISLAM'S ENCOUNTER WITH MODERN SCIENCE

A Mismatch Made in Heaven

Taner Edis
Truman State University

CAMBRIDGE
UNIVERSITY PRESS

CAMBRIDGE
UNIVERSITY PRESS

Shaftesbury Road, Cambridge CB2 8EA, United Kingdom

One Liberty Plaza, 20th Floor, New York, NY 10006, USA

477 Williamstown Road, Port Melbourne, VIC 3207, Australia

314–321, 3rd Floor, Plot 3, Splendor Forum, Jasola District Centre, New Delhi – 110025, India

103 Penang Road, #05–06/07, Visioncrest Commercial, Singapore 238467

Cambridge University Press is part of Cambridge University Press & Assessment, a department of the University of Cambridge.

We share the University's mission to contribute to society through the pursuit of education, learning and research at the highest international levels of excellence.

www.cambridge.org
Information on this title: www.cambridge.org/9781009478649

DOI: 10.1017/9781009257473

First published 2023

A catalogue record for this publication is available from the British Library

ISBN 978-1-009-47864-9 Hardback
ISBN 978-1-009-25744-2 Paperback
ISSN 2754-7094 (online)
ISSN 2754-7086 (print)

Islam's Encounter with Modern Science

A Mismatch Made in Heaven

Elements in Islam and Science

DOI: 10.1017/9781009257473
First published online: November 2023

Taner Edis
Truman State University
Author for correspondence: Taner Edis, edis@truman.edu

Abstract: Within Muslim populations, debates about the compatibility between science and religion tend to be framed by the long-standing competition between modernizing reformers, particularly westernizers, and theological conservatives. Much like their liberal Christian counterparts, reformers propose to embrace technical knowledge and reinterpret traditional beliefs undermined by modern science. Conservatives are more open to challenging the content of science, especially when science appears to support materialist views. Islamists promote an alternative, non-Western style of modernity, nurturing a more pious professional class that contrasts with westernized elites. By scientific standards, westernizers appear to have the upper hand, especially as conservative apologetics is drawn toward distortions of science such as creationism, or fruitless attempts to Islamize science. But conservatives can also point to some success in defusing tensions between scientific and religious institutions without adopting the full secularization of science seen in post-Christian countries.

This Element also has a video abstract: www.cambridge.org/edis_abstract

Keywords: Islam, science and Islam, westernization, Islamic creationism, materialism, science and religion

ISBNs: 9781009478649 (HB), 9781009257442 (PB), 9781009257473 (OC)
ISSNs: 2754-7094 (online), 2754-7086 (print)

Contents

1 Why Science Matters

1.1 The Scientific Religion

Long ago, when I lived in Baltimore, the slogan "Baltimore: the city that reads" started appearing on park benches and other public surfaces. Baltimore had been found to have a high rate of functional illiteracy, which must have been embarrassing to civic leaders. Hence the slogan: it did not really announce that denizens of Baltimore were enthusiastic readers, but the opposite. "The city that reads" expressed an aspiration, not a reality. It signaled a vague determination to do something about an acknowledged problem.

Before I landed in Baltimore for graduate school, I grew up in Turkey. There, political and cultural leaders were concerned about how Turkey lagged in science and technology. It still lags behind. Indeed, all Muslim countries do (Guessoum and Osama 2015a; Guessoum and Osama 2015b). Many Muslim intellectuals, who often think of Islam as a civilization as well as a faith, worry that Muslims always seem backward in science. Therefore, some are apt to declare a perfect harmony between Islam and science. Islam is supposed to be a scientific religion, the most rational of the Abrahamic faiths. The Prophet encouraged the pursuit of knowledge, and in the early Islamic empires, when piety was purer, Muslims enjoyed a Golden Age of scientific accomplishment. Not only did Islam promote scientific investigation, science was practically a religious duty (Akhter 2009; Al-Hassani, Woodcock, and Saoud 2012).

As in "Baltimore: the city that reads," such proclamations reveal aspirations rather than realities. Muslims not only lag in science, they often have difficulties reconciling science and faith. Modern science has raised questions about the supernatural beliefs endorsed by all world religions. Muslims have also had to face such challenges (Edis 2007). And for most Muslims, science, however valued, remains an import from foreign lands.

Pronouncements about the harmony between science and Islam also overlook deep divisions among Muslims. Many Muslim elites have favored extensive modernization of Muslim institutions and practices. Indeed, some modernizing reformers are best described as westernizers, urging Muslims to follow Western examples in culture as well as in technical accomplishments. Reformers typically affirm the compatibility of Islam and science, but they imagine an Islam purified of what they think of as medieval superstitions. For those most enthusiastic about Western modernity, science comes first, and religion has to adapt. More conservative Muslims also want to acquire science and are enthusiastic about technology. But they will quickly add that the glorious design revealed in creation can only fortify the faith of the believers. Traditional supernatural beliefs are not negotiable, and science must support such beliefs. Many

Muslims, naturally, find merit in both modernizing and conservative positions, and hope to steer a moderate course. Debates about science and religion, however, are often framed by the opposition between westernizing and conservative poles.

I come from a secular, westernizing background, and I have never been a believer. My views on Islam are those of an outsider to the faith. Still, like many of my more devout friends who also went into science and engineering, I have had to face questions about science in Muslim lands. After all, everyone agrees that Muslims have not yet succeeded at modern science. Westernizers, tradition-minded conservatives, and Islamists will join in deploring the poor state of science and technology in the Muslim world. Muslim countries have low research productivity (Haq and Tanveer 2020). Very few well-known scientists are Muslim. Nobel laureates in the sciences, for example, include only Mohammad Abdus Salam (physics 1979), Ahmed Zewail (chemistry 1999), and Aziz Sancar (chemistry 2015). Abdus Salam, who belonged to the Ahmadi sect, is not even considered legally Muslim in his native Pakistan. More important, all did their scientific work outside of Muslim lands, in the post-Christian West. Today, it is easy to encounter diversity and inclusion-inspired pictures of lab workers in headscarves. Such images paper over how individual Muslim scientists are bit players in global enterprises detached from any local culture. Muslims do not set the research agendas. Islam does not contribute to the picture of the universe drawn by our sciences. In the lab, Islam is an irrelevance.

In the natural sciences such as physics, chemistry, and biology, the Muslim presence is so unremarkable that if aliens were to abduct all Muslims from all the labs of the world, the global scientific enterprise would hardly be affected. If all Jewish scientists were to mysteriously disappear, it would be impossible not to notice. Again, among Muslims, such an observation is not controversial. All factions agree that Muslim contributions to science in modern times have been unimpressive. Almost everyone thinks that *science matters*, and that poor performance is a collective problem, even an embarrassment, for the world of Islam.

The direct causes of underperformance are clear enough. After all, scientific research is expensive, and most Muslim countries are not rich. They occupy a subordinate role in the global economy and often have a poorly educated labor force (Akhtar 2018; Kuru 2019: 62–63). Many Muslim lands have industrialized, but the high end of technology development, together with cutting-edge natural science, takes place elsewhere. Almost all Muslim countries were subjected to colonialism, and today operate under what is in many respects a neocolonial economic order.

In that case, a proper evaluation of Muslim scientific production would compare countries in a similar economic position. Then, it turns out that while Muslims still underperform, their deficit in science is smaller. Middle- and lower-income countries tend to invest more in the applied sciences – engineering, medicine – that promise immediate benefits. Particularly when applied science is included, middle-income Muslim countries have a scientific production roughly on a par with similarly situated non-Muslim countries. Turkey, Malaysia, and Indonesia have taken advantage of the deindustrialization of the post-Christian West to achieve middle-income status, and their contribution to science and technology is comparable to other recently industrialized countries with similar per capita incomes. Their officials and academics often focus on concerns such as advancing their countries' position in a knowledge economy. Underperformance in science education, for example, is a practical worry for businesses, not just a deficit in national prestige associated with a lag in natural science (Aysan et al. 2018; Hill, Khan, and Zhuang 2012).

There is, naturally, considerable variation. Iran, laboring under economic strangulation by the United States, still sustains a respectable scientific enterprise and entertains ambitions in biotechnology (Fard, Moslemy, and Golshahi 2013; Soofi and Ghazinoory 2013). Iran's performance perhaps reflects its traditional position as a center of intellectual activity in the Islamic world. Arab countries do not do very well. Political instability and failed states do not make good conditions for scientific work. Oil-producing countries are rich, but they do not support the broad technical expertise more diverse economies require (Kuru 2019: 48–52; Mydin, Askari, and Mirakhor 2018).

Still, even if poor scientific performance reflects underdevelopment, Muslims wonder why they find themselves in such a predicament. After all, why should Muslims, who possess a scientific religion, and whose superior faith should grant them an unparalleled insight into how the universe functions, be left behind in the first place? Reformers often blame religious conservatism; conservatives suspect that insufficient piety is at the root of all Muslim troubles. Whatever is responsible, there is then the question of what is to be done, especially in cases where modern knowledge appears to contradict traditional beliefs. Among reformers, westernizers want to separate science from religion, sometimes going so far as recognizing the authority of revelation only in matters of abstruse metaphysics and personal morality. Islamists envision an Islam-friendly science operating in a pious society, and have competing visions for how to achieve such a goal. In any case, Muslims confront questions about modern science and their religion. Are traditional supernatural beliefs compatible with scientific knowledge? Is Islam an impediment to doing science?

Debates about Islam and science center on elite forms of knowledge. Science, after all, belongs to highly trained specialists. Scientific knowledge then diffuses though the population via education and the media, under the guidance of educated professionals. In this respect, science is similar to official theologies propagated by a specialized class of religious scholars. Questions about science and religion are not just fuel for intellectual debate. They also involve opportunities for competition and cooperation between elite institutions.

To further complicate matters, religion has a strong populist element. In most Muslim countries, an officially sanctioned version of Islam coexists in tension with multiple sects, revival movements, and popular supernatural beliefs that overflow orthodox channels. Religious movements may come to enjoy political power and reshape theology. And in turn, representatives of official religion can draw on popular support to impose their views about science. Modernizing reformers can't make such populist appeals. But they still have to worry about whether popular religion will be an obstacle to producing a scientifically educated population. The relationship of science and Islam, then, involves more than knowledge claims propagated by elites. How ordinary believers respond to scientific and religious controversies is just as important (Edis 2007).

Muslim populations are typically more devout than the mostly secular citizens of technologically advanced post-Christian countries. This does not mean religiously orthodox conformity. Rival religious movements promote varied attitudes toward science or technology. Different movements also have different ways of relating to historical memories of classical Islamic civilization, even as traditional beliefs continue to define a common ideal.

Muslims, even though they have widely varying levels of religious observance, very often understand the world in supernatural terms. For example, after an earthquake or tsunami in a Muslim country, some preachers will announce that the disaster was a divine punishment. After all, the Quran has many verses in which insufficiently faithful peoples are punished through disasters. Surveys show that much of the population will agree that natural events reflect supernatural purposes (Aksa 2020; Chester, Duncan, and Al Ghasyah Dhanhani 2013). Muslims typically believe in jinn, invisible spirits who can interact with humans and cause mischief. Religious leaders affirm the reality of jinn, citing Quranic verses. They may offer to help believers who think they may be attacked or possessed by jinn (El-Zein 2009; Rassool 2019).

Such a magical, supernatural view of the world runs deeper than popular superstitions. Muslims often resist Darwinian evolution, not just because the Quran endorses the special creation of humans, but also because Muslim intellectual culture usually suggests that the intricate design of lifeforms is prime evidence for a creator (Edis 2009). Alongside modern medicine,

Muslim patients often favor traditional treatments such as cupping, leeches, and exorcisms of jinn through chanting Quranic verses. Such practices, sometimes called "prophetic medicine," attract customers partly because they are supposed to be more Islamically authentic. Many pseudoscientific enterprises attempt to combine such traditional medical practices with an image of modern expertise (Hussein, Albar, and Alsanad 2019; Sax 2020; Stiedenroth 2020).

The encounter between Islam and modern science, then, does not just generate apologetic literature, competing theological interpretations, and academic controversies. Very often, projects of reconciling religion and science are connected to religious movements and a popular religious marketplace of ideas and practices. Especially when they lack strong connections to scientific institutions and westernized elites, such religious movements promote distortions of science. Slogans asserting harmony between science and Islam do not just express aspirations. They also conceal a serious mismatch between how modern science and traditional Islam describe our world.

1.2 Losing the Golden Age

Arguments that Islam encourages science invariably look back to a Golden Age of Muslim science. Between the ninth and thirteenth centuries, empires ruled by Muslims hosted the strongest intellectual communities in the world. Both the material wealth of Muslim elites, and the number of volumes in their libraries, were incomparably greater than the barbarians in Western Europe.

Naturally, this period has inspired religious and nationalist mythmaking. Stories about a Golden Age function as a proof of concept of the affinity between Islam and science. Past glories may yet be revived. Therefore, medieval philosophers and investigators who may have found little recognition in their lifetimes now appear as heroes in textbooks. In some accounts, Muslims are supposed to have laid the groundwork for or anticipated much of later European science and technology (Al-Hassani, Woodcock, and Saoud 2012; Kollu and Han 2022; for criticism see Brentjes, Edis, and Richter-Bernburg 2016; Elshakry 2020).

For example, in many Arab countries, the ninth-century Andalusian Ibn Firnas is celebrated for achieving flight. Most Turks believe that in the seventeenth century, Hezarfen Ahmet Çelebi flew across the Bosporus. Both stories are based on untrustworthy sources and have details that seem closer to sorcery than technology. And flight with artificial wings powered by arm muscles is physically impossible. Such myths have even spread outside Muslim countries, endorsed by books, traveling museum exhibits, and online resources. Muslims, apparently, invented much of what led to modern technology, but then inexplicably failed to follow through (Edis and Bix 2016).

There is no doubt that the early Muslim empires inherited the knowledge built up by the civilizations of antiquity, developed it further, and produced the best medieval examples of what, in hindsight, we would call natural science. Nonetheless, medieval knowledge – in Christendom as well as in Muslim lands – was different from modern science. Medieval bestiaries would include fantastic creatures, astronomy and mathematics were entwined with astrology, and medical texts recommended magical practices as well as describing useful surgical techniques. Some medieval science practiced in Muslim lands, such as optics, showed signs of developing an experimental approach coupled to mathematical modeling. Selectively emphasizing what appears similar to today's science, however, overlooks the overall intellectual context of medieval knowledge. The Muslim precursor of science never abandoned a supernatural framework where divine intentions and magical influences were pervasive. Mystical philosophies or astrology had a much stronger influence on intellectual life than abortive attempts at developing optics. Even when practically oriented, Muslim science had only tenuous links to technological advancement (Blake 2016, Saif et al. 2021).

Just as important, Muslim intellectual practices never led to a properly institutionalized enterprise of experimental investigation coupled to theoretical explanation. Most of the kinds of knowledge Muslims inherited from antiquity were considered "foreign sciences." Compared to the religious sciences, these foreign sciences enjoyed lesser prestige. Some, such as medicine, were practically useful and worthy of pursuit. Others, however, were more closely associated with Greek philosophy. And philosophy, although theistic, harbored a tendency toward doubting revelation. Muslim orthodoxy, particularly in the dominant Sunni tradition, developed in a manner that encouraged suspicion of speculative philosophy (Aydın 2021a; Hassan 2020).

Much of medieval science, together with philosophy, therefore never found a stable institutional home. Almost all premodern Muslim learning depended on informal associations of scholars. Nonetheless, madrassa education produced a shared intellectual background for the class of religious scholars. This education emphasized the religious sciences, particularly the interpretation of sacred texts and the production of appropriate legal rulings. Even theology had a secondary status. While the foreign sciences were never excluded from Muslim intellectual life, their propagation almost entirely depended on sparse networks of scholars who happened to have a personal interest. For classical Muslim civilization, the precursors of natural science existed on the periphery of intellectual life (Huff 2017; Dallal 2010 complicates this picture).

Medieval Christian science was broadly similar; if anything, it was less impressive. In that case, why did modern science emerge from the backwaters of Western Europe and not Muslim lands, or perhaps China? Historians of science do not have a clear consensus on an explanation. But it appears that no single factor is responsible – not any major feature of intellectual life in any medieval civilization.

Certainly, some aspects of Muslim intellectual tradition impeded natural science (Huff 2017). For example, Muslims were often drawn toward occasionalism, which denied natural causality in order to emphasize the complete dependence of everything on a divine will. And yet, a rigid occasionalism was never the only metaphysical option for Muslim thinkers. Moreover, the Muslim ambivalence about philosophy could have encouraged investigators to set metaphysics aside and develop a more practical, experimental science. Some premodern Muslim thinkers decoupled natural science from religious and metaphysical concerns (Dallal 2010). That such intellectual options did not generate a modern scientific enterprise is probably due to historical accidents rather than anything central to Islam.

Historians still debate whether the science practiced in Muslim empires began to stagnate, or even decline (Dallal 2010; Kuru 2019: 104–07). In any event, the continued development of Muslim science took place slowly, within its medieval, supernatural framework. Western Europe, in contrast, witnessed the explosion of an experimental and mathematically formulated physical science that joined curiosity-driven investigations with relentless technological advances. This new variety of science carved out an intellectual and institutional space that became increasingly independent of both orthodox supernaturalism and popular magical beliefs. The Muslim form of science never achieved a similar lift-off (Huff 2011).

Muslim elites became keenly aware of the new science in the eighteenth century, after Europeans inflicted catastrophic defeats on Muslim empires such as the Ottomans and Mughal India. The Western European barbarians set out to trade with and to colonize the globe. The superior military and commercial prowess of the Western Christians was associated with the new forms of knowledge they had developed (Livingston 2018a).

Rulers of Muslim lands tried to adapt, both by attempting to revive a purer state of their religion and by embracing change. A new, more disciplined military organization was crucial, as was a more efficient imperial bureaucracy. And since European power was linked to their superior knowledge, it behooved Muslims to learn what was useful from the new science.

The new science, however, kept growing explosively, contributing to the Industrial Revolution and further colonialism. During the nineteenth century,

Muslim power rapidly receded, and elites could no longer invest their hopes in religious revival or tinkering around the edges of medieval institutions. Some westernization was inescapable, and assimilating the new science had to be an important component of the effort to become more modern. Once again, militaries and imperial bureaucracies led the way, installing a modern state apparatus and introducing modern education, including science and technology, starting with the children of elites. Science mattered, and it mattered because it was key to military and economic survival (Burçak 2008; Kalın 2002).

Whether in Iran, the Ottoman Middle East, or the Indian subcontinent under British domination, a common feature of the nineteenth- and early-twentieth-century intellectual landscape became calls for a revival of rationality and science within Islam. The old practices had gone stagnant, and the religious scholars had become too set in their ways. Moreover, Muslims did not just need to absorb the new learning and adapt it to their lands. Since the new scientific knowledge continued to grow at a fast pace, catching up to the modern world required that Muslims should learn how to practice science and not be continually left behind as the frontiers of knowledge advanced. Some traditionally educated religious scholars embraced reform and some took reactionary positions. But Muslim lands also started developing a stratum of elites who had a modern education. They usually supported reform (Masud 2009).

Some of today's factions – conservatives, westernizers – already appear at the beginning of the debates about Islam and modern science. Almost everyone agreed that some modernization was necessary, but how far should reforms go? Importing useful knowledge was not enough. But to actively produce new knowledge, how much of the modern culture associated with Western science needed to be assimilated? To save Muslim civilization, how much exposure to the suspect morals and religious deviations of the modern world could be tolerated? Reformers were willing to interfere with traditional religion in order to protect what they thought was essential to Islam. Conservatives insisted that importing science should not extend to corrupting religion.

To further complicate matters, in the late nineteenth century, after Darwin, Christendom faced an intensified confrontation between scientific and traditionally religious descriptions of the world. As a result, together with science, Muslims imported the Western debate about science versus supernatural religion. A handful of extreme westernizers even toyed with the science-inspired materialist philosophies emerging in Europe (Hanioğlu 2008). They were easily suppressed, but among westernizers, the notion of a conflict between science and religion lingered. Science mattered, science was a necessity. But Western science, it seemed, also harbored a potential threat.

1.3 Responding to Science

Muslims were not the only ones to struggle to come to terms with the modern world. Western Europe and its settler societies, where modernity started and picked up steam, became accustomed to social and cultural upheavals. Where colonial powers penetrated, novel economic relationships, modern military practices, and subversive political ideals followed. And somehow entangled with the promises and problems of modernity, maybe even driving it all, was the new science.

Russian, Chinese, and Japanese intellectuals of the nineteenth century also worried about modernizing without losing their cultural distinctions. Buddhists and Hindus also had to respond to a science that was taking an increasingly materialist direction, removing signs of spirit and purpose from nature (Brown 2020). Even Western Christians were uneasy. On one hand, imperial success could signal the triumph of a suitably modernized Christianity and its ideals of progress. On the other hand, modern institutions tended toward independence from religion. Science, Christians hoped, could affirm a spiritual and moral order in nature. But science also contained a potential for mischief.

Across the world, elites started demanding more modern, less pervasively religious forms of education for their offspring. Intellectuals asked if their societies could follow the example of the Christian West without too many of the accompanying cultural dislocations. Usually, they expected that religion would still underwrite the social order, provided it adapted to the times. Science was a very useful tool, but it had to be used with care.

Many intellectuals, however, sought a new freedom in the disruptions of modernity. Some came to expect national salvation through capitalist ideologies of progress; others were captivated by the aspiration to an alternative modernity represented by the political left (Sing 2018). Science, in any case, would light the path, whether by the technologies unleashed by captains of industry, or by an allegedly scientific socialism. In more liberal and left-wing circles, science became not just a source of doubt about the supernatural, but part of a more comprehensive critique of religious ways of life.

Even conservative religious responses to science and modernity became marked by doubt as a viable option. Religious fundamentalism, for example, is a modern phenomenon. A literal interpretation of sacred texts becomes more popular when the texts are available to a wider, more literate population. For fundamentalists, scripture no longer belongs to a mythic, sacred reality that stands apart from the everyday world. Stories become history, and statements in sacred texts come to express concrete facts like the facts of science (Bruce 2008: 12–14).

Modernizing interpretations of sacred texts are also products of an intellectual culture shaped by the new science. When confronted with an embarrassing passage, a fundamentalist might insist that it is nonetheless true, just like a scientific fact. A theological modernist might interpret the text more metaphorically, perhaps turning it into a vehicle for a moral message. But such metaphors start becoming mere literary metaphors. The sense that sacred texts present deeper, more solid truths than those of the seen world, that mere material existence is patterned by the primary reality of the spiritual realm, starts to fade away.

All these tendencies exist within Islam today. Indeed, there is very little that is unique about Muslim responses to modern science eroding the credibility of supernatural claims. Almost every apologetic maneuver, every theological evasion, every scriptural reinterpretation has a Christian parallel. Every pseudo-scientific enterprise, every conspiracy theory favored by Muslims has echoes among Jews, Hindus, or Buddhists. For centuries now, intellectuals belonging to every world religion have felt torn between ambitions to achieve a pious version of modernity and suspicions that nothing less than restoration of a bygone age will do.

Naturally, the details of how Muslims attempt to protect their faith can be very different. Muslims believe the Quran is divine revelation, not the Bible, and so they will defend different stories. Compared to Christians, conservative Muslims are loyal to different conceptions of social and sexual morality, and their revealed truths support a distinctly Muslim social order. But modern science challenges *all* traditional supernatural claims (Edis 2002). Modern social and economic life strains *all* revealed moralities.

Muslim positions on science and religion, then, are distinctive not because of their content but their context. Western Christians can claim to have ushered in modernity, even if they wish it had not spun out of control. The corrosive doubt inadvertently encouraged by modern knowledge may be unfortunate, but it is an outgrowth of a Christian intellectual culture. For Muslims, in contrast, Western technological modernity has been a foreign import. The new science, in its relentless advance, has highlighted how Muslims have constantly needed to play catch-up. Some reformers have seen opportunity in change, but for most conservative Muslims science has too often been one of the forces that fragmented Muslim civilization. The skepticism that often accompanies science has not been an internally generated heresy that became increasingly hard to contain. Instead, it has been an external imposition (Edis 2007).

During much of the twentieth century, conservative Muslim reactions to science might have seemed of little consequence. After all, the reformers had the upper hand. The last independent Muslim empire, the Ottomans, succumbed to the colonial powers. But then, the Anatolian Turks successfully fought for their independence. The new Turkish leadership imposed an ambitious program of westernization on their territory. The Turkish Revolution of the 1920s attempted to purify Islam by reducing the faith to a core that concerned personal identity and ritual practice, rather than public matters of law or politics. Influenced by materialist and secularizing currents of thought, the revolutionaries trusted in science and modern education. And since they wanted a culture that sustained modernity and constantly created novelty, they even favored Western forms of art and music. The Turkish Republic aimed to be a secular state that would nurture the best science and technology, while a depoliticized Islam would still reign over the personal lives of its citizens (Berkes 1998; Kuru and Stepan 2012).

As other Muslim countries attained independence after the Second World War, their elites leaned toward secular nationalism. No one matched the Turkish revolutionaries in their anti-clerical fervor. But the nationalists still attempted to tame traditional authorities such as the religious scholars. Secular law took precedence over an Islamic law mostly restricted to personal matters. By mid-century, many Western observers expected a continually diminishing role for Islam in public life.

That did not happen. In the last fifty years, political Islam has captured the imagination of many Muslims worldwide. A variety of political Islam that has taken power in large, middle-income countries – Turkey, Malaysia, Indonesia – is particularly important. Such Islamists have taken the fate of Western Christianity as a bad example to avoid, and vigorously opposed secularism and cultural westernization. They have tended toward fundamentalism. But such Islamists have also been inspired by the United States as a wealthy, but conservative, power. They have promoted an ardently capitalist, populist, and publicly religious politics. And they have won elections by promising worldly success for Muslims, uniting political and religious salvation. After the collapse of the political left, they have offered their own, more pious form of alternative modernity (Edis 2016).

Today's Islamists are likely to be enthusiastic about technology and about all forms of modern expertise that lead to economic rewards. They are cooler toward natural science. Indeed, they represent a third option to relate science and religion, beyond a more traditional conservatism and westernization. The Islamist ideal of pious modernity decouples science and technology, downplaying science while affirming technology and economic growth.

In any case, Islamists have enjoyed political success. They set the context of the relationship between science and Islam today. Debates about science and religion are often framed as contests between theological options, scholarly analyses, or scientists' interpretations of their faith. But a context shaped by political Islam encourages suspicion of educated elites, and favors media-friendly presentations over more academic forms of discourse (Edis 2020a). Such an environment also affects which scholars enjoy influence. For better or for worse, Islam encounters science through popular apologetics as much as through intellectually serious proposals.

2 Conflicts of Content

2.1 Scientific Miracles in the Quran

If the affinity between science and Islam is not to remain an aspirational slogan, it should eventually require some evidence. That should not be too difficult. After all, Muslims usually believe that our existence expresses a divine purpose, and that the universe has a supernatural design. It would be no surprise, then, if revelations from the creator should also manifest an exact knowledge of our universe.

Many Muslims are convinced that just such evidence is available. A popular form of Islamic apologetics claims that modern science and technology can be found prefigured in the Quran (Bigliardi 2017; Naguib 2019; Telliel 2019). Scattered verses contain hints about how nature works that could not have been known to Arabs in the sixth century. These scientific miracles in the Quran show that the sacred text is not a mere human composition: it must have a divine source. Far from challenging faith, modern science confirms the truth of Islam.

According to such apologetics, the Quran refers to the expansion of the universe. After all, 21:30 says that heaven and earth were once joined and then separated. 51:47 speaks of how the creator expanded the heavens. More earthly aspects of science, such as the water cycle, appear in verses such as 39:21, describing the divine power that sends down rain and makes waters flow. Even minor details show up, such as 25:53 that describes two seas, salty and fresh, separated from one another. Obviously, this must refer to the salinity barrier between the Mediterranean and the Atlantic.

The Quran is supposed to present accurate embryological information when it describes how a drop of semen progresses to become a clot and then flesh, in 23:12–14 and other verses (Guénon 2019). In numerous verses, the Quran refers to seven heavens. Various interpreters find all sorts of details of modern astrophysics in the seven layers of sky: galaxies, perhaps, or the hidden dimensions postulated by string theory, or dark matter and dark energy. No one in the sixth century could have known about such things. Apologists then proceed to calculate the speed of light from Quranic verses, suggest that stories about the miracles of Solomon hint that airplanes are possible, and find evidence of atoms and nuclear energy in revelation. Biology, geology, physics, and chemistry: they are all there in the Quran (Nurbaki 2022 [1985]; Sayksa and Arni 2016).

The notion that all knowledge is linked to the Quran has deep roots. But proclaiming that science can be found in sacred texts is a distinctly modern form of apologetics. Highly educated Muslims might find the interpretations to be forced, associating this style of apologetics with televangelists and a lower-class style of religiosity. And many a conservative scholar will dismiss newfangled readings in favor of interpretations established during the classical period of Islam (Çalışkan 2020; Sardar 2011: 356–57). And yet, finding science in the Quran is very popular, surfacing in innumerable books, pamphlets, websites, and online videos that reassure Muslims that their religion is correct.

Arguing that modern science and technology is prefigured in the Quran goes back at least to the early twentieth century, when some religious scholars explored more modern interpretations of their texts and encouraged Muslims to pursue the new sciences (Livingston 2018b). Indeed, such apologetics became the signature of some influential modernizing religious movements. The Nur movement in Turkey, for example, promoted economic development and technological modernity, encouraging the religious leadership of engineers and businessmen as much as more traditional scholars. Starting with popular magazines that claimed science supported Islam, they pioneered an apologetics style that turned out to be perfectly suited to the internet era (Mardin 1989; Markham and Sayılgan 2017).

In the second half of the twentieth century, apologetics claiming that science supported religion became commonplace throughout the Muslim world. In premodern times, popular Islam tended to have a lot of local variation, assimilating regional supernatural beliefs and propagating miracle stories featuring the local Sufi saints. Today's globalized Islam has erased many of these differences. Scripture has become more directly available to individual believers, strengthening more fundamentalist attitudes. Modern systems of public education have made science the authority about facts of nature. Naturally, popular religion has come to combine science and traditional beliefs. If Western scientists would acknowledge the scientific miracles in the Quran, that would be best. In the late twentieth century, figures such as Maurice Bucaille, a French medical doctor, became central actors in the developing international apologetic of finding science in the Quran (Bigliardi 2011).

And once interpreters start looking for it, scientific miracles associated with Islam appear beyond the Quran. For example, the prophetic traditions include many stories concerning health and disease, including episodes where the Prophet performs healings. Magical practices are common, as in the story where Muhammad advises that if a housefly falls in a drink, it should be fully dipped in, because one of its wings has a disease and the other the cure (Bukhari 4:537). Among many Muslims today, fake scientific medical practices that have an Islamic pedigree are popular, especially if they can be linked with sacred texts. Muslim medical professionals regularly publish papers affirming both pseudoscientific practices and scientific miracles in the Quran (Orayj 2022).

According to any scholarly standard, efforts to have scientific miracles validate Islam are embarrassments. Fundamentalist approaches to reconciling sacred texts with modern knowledge are not promising. Indeed, the problem is not just a text getting some facts wrong. Large parts of the Muslim sacred texts are remarkably opaque and open to interpretation. A handful of errors could be interpreted away. The deeper problem is that it is *not* difficult to understand many of the scientifically dubious statements in sacred texts. Consider, for example, Quranic pronouncements about the seven heavens or the seven layers of skies. This is a notable feature of the universe as imagined by the Quran, further elaborated in traditions such as those about the Night Journey of the Prophet. There is nothing remotely similar to seven layers of sky in today's astrophysics. But at the time of the Quran, the appropriate cosmology would have included Ptolemaic astronomy, which featured seven celestial spheres associated with the Sun, Moon, and the visible planets (Janos 2012).

The Quran also contains fossilized relics of even older Near Eastern cosmologies, with a flat Earth below and a solid firmament stretched above. When the Quran alludes to the divine spreading out of the surface of the Earth, held in place by mountains like tent pegs, it refers to ancient beliefs, not the expanding universe of today's astrophysics (Wright 2000).

The alleged embryology in the Quran is an echo of the medicine of antiquity (Elsakaan and Longo 2016). Magical healing in the prophetic traditions is ancient superstition. The universe of the sacred texts is an archaic conception, a stage for miracle stories about biblical figures such as Moses, Solomon, and Jesus. Divine power is manifested in resurrections, magic, and talking animals.

The modern tendency toward fundamentalism only amplifies the conflict with modern science invited by such an overall picture. At face value, the sacred texts assume a framework of a high god, angels, demons, lesser spirits such as jinn, and relate the adventures of prophets and miracle-workers. They speak of a heaven and hell, and a possibly imminent apocalypse and judgment. In such a thoroughly supernatural framework, divine purpose and design works as a genuine explanation rather than a metaphysical assertion – traditional beliefs *make sense*. But when taken literally, almost nothing in such a framework fits modern scientific understandings of how the universe works.

There is a stark conflict between ancient conceptions of the world in which supernatural agency makes sense and our modern sciences where nature works on its own. This is a serious difficulty for every religious tradition. Christians faced this challenge first, as advancing historical and natural scientific knowledge made it increasingly difficult to accept a universe infused with supernatural purpose in every detail. Some theologians responded by turning to fundamentalism, others resorted to more obscure interpretations of traditional beliefs. Today, conservative Christian scholars still defend supernatural explanations of both ancient and contemporary miracle stories (Keener 2011). But they do so as intellectual rebels, aware that in the secularized intellectual high culture of today's wealthy post-Christian countries, belief in miracles or literally understood Bible stories is no longer respectable.

Among Muslims, setting overt supernaturalism aside has also been difficult. With economic development, folk varieties of Islam are giving way to more globalized, more scripture-focused forms of Islam, dampening beliefs in the miracles performed by local saints (van Bruinessen 2009). But such changes have led to even more emphasis on the supernatural beliefs embedded in the sacred texts.

Muslims have always been drawn toward adopting the parts of science that are useful while rejecting aspects that are culturally dangerous. Belief in scientific miracles in the Quran promises just such a resolution. Indeed, if not to a similar extent, some Christians have also thought that modern science might be prefigured in the Bible. Hindu nationalists are also famous for finding science and technology in their sacred texts (Nanda 2016). But the Muslim temptation to affirm scriptural miracles may be stronger. The Quran is more central to Islam than the Bible is to Christianity or Judaism. Almost every Muslim believes that the Quran is a direct divine communication. And if the Quran best makes sense in an archaic framework where supernatural forces are palpably real, Muslims will naturally reinterpret their faith to both affirm their texts and find science in the Quran.

2.2 Staying within Physics

Science is not just a set of facts, and scientists do not collect facts like stamps. Modern science is notable for its ambitious conceptual frameworks – overarching theories about how the world works – such as relativity, quantum mechanics, or evolution. These are not mere theories in the colloquial sense; such theoretical frameworks are universal and fundamental statements about the universe. Science makes progress when it achieves positive feedback loops that let its experiments and theories correct one another, providing evidence that the conceptual frameworks at work are at least good approximations to reality.

In the nineteenth century, when Muslims became acquainted with Western debates over science and religion, they encountered materialist attempts to fashion an overall framework. Darwinian evolution provoked the strongest controversy, but nineteenth-century materialism was most inspired by the physical science of the day. Life, it seemed, might eventually be understood within the laws of physics. Human minds, perhaps, would also be assimilated into a picture where nature worked according to rigid, impersonal rules of cause and effect (Gregory 1977; Olson 2008). A miracle would be a violation of those rules.

For Christians, such a concept of miracles could be welcome. After all, a miracle would then not just be a spectacular display of power but a clear sign of something beyond nature. Materialists, however, thought of divine intervention as an arbitrary, improbable intrusion into the well-established natural order. Muslims first interpreted this debate in terms of their own intellectual tradition, which favored forms of occasionalism that made the divine will directly responsible for everything. The few early Muslim responses to materialism revisited metaphysical debates within Islamic philosophical theology (Bulğen 2019), but only superficially engaged with the new scientific developments that inspired the European materialists.

The more interesting reactions to materialism came from the Christian West, where some tried to turn science against materialism. Psychical researchers in the nineteenth century hoped to establish the primary reality of spirit by scientific means. A quest for paranormal phenomena became established on the fringes of science. Psychic feats became the new miracles, indicating a realm of freedom beyond the rules that determined the behavior of mere matter. The prospect of paranormal realities attracted religious thinkers who favored a more individualist spirituality that could escape both the dogmas of the established religions and the hopelessness of materialism (Lachapelle 2011; Oppenheim 1985).

Relativity and quantum mechanics, which physicists ushered in during the first half of the twentieth century, complicated matters. Until then, debates about materialism took commonsense conceptions of matter, causality, and the laws of nature for granted. The revolutions in physics unsettled all of that, producing a picture of a universe where commonsense notions were useful only in the very limited environment of our everyday experience. Relativity violated our intuitions about time and space. Quantum mechanics revealed a world where our everyday sense of order and causality was erected on a substrate of microscopic randomness.

Some Christians and Muslims have thought that quantum mechanics could allow miracles that did not violate the laws of physics – divine interventions might be hidden in the statistical noise (Russell 2009; Taslaman 2008; for criticism see Edis 2019). But the most enthusiastic support for the notion that the new physics re-enchanted the world has come from religious movements outside the mainstream of monotheism, often associated with occult spiritualities and the religions of the Indian subcontinent. To New Agers and similar enthusiasts, it has seemed that the new physics broke the materialist framework of rigid rules. It allowed for the paranormal.

Parapsychologists, descendants of the psychical researchers, often argue that quantum physics suggests that consciousness is the fundamental reality. But parapsychologists have never been able to convince the mainstream scientific community that psychic phenomena are real (Edis 2018b; Reber and Alcock 2020). Nonetheless, both psychic claims and mystical views that take inspiration from quantum physics remain popular. In the post-Christian West, paranormal belief is a main feature of alternative, individualist spiritualities. In India, quantum mysticism has found support from Hindu nationalists and has established a presence even in higher education (Geraci 2018; Nanda 2003).

So far, Muslims have shown no comparable interest in using modern physics for apologetic purposes. Some Muslims with a physics background have argued that Islam is compatible with modern physics, or at least that physics does not demand materialism (Bigliardi 2014; Guessoum 2010). However, they have only rarely endorsed the large-scale distortions of physics required for quantum mysticism. There are crank attempts to make physical predictions using "Islamic science" (Jaafar and Wahiddin 2016), but they attract little attention, even among conservative Muslim apologists.

Popular media in Muslim lands often embraces psychics and uses the word "quantum" to mean magic. Many Muslims believe in psychic powers and ask religious scholars how such powers may be understood in the context of traditional Islamic beliefs. But the connection between paranormal claims and popular Islam is superficial, comparable to the way that reports of encounters with space aliens also attract attention and provoke questions about jinn. Apologists who argue that science supports traditional Islam will occasionally borrow from the global subculture of paranormal beliefs and quantum mysticism to score points against materialism (Tarhan 2021 [2008]). Nonetheless, for popular Muslim apologetics, abuse of modern physics is rarely a main theme.

One possible exception is Sufi-inspired literature that appeals to educated, professional-class seekers and potential converts, both in urban environments in Muslim lands and in the post-Christian West. But westernized neo-Sufi beliefs tend to be uprooted from Islamic tradition and hardly distinguishable from the derivatives of Hindu or Buddhist spiritualities that also appeal to an upmarket clientele (Soyubol 2021). The tendency toward deification of individual consciousness apparent in paranormal mysticism usually does not sit well with the strict monotheism demanded by more conservative varieties of Islam.

The Muslim response to physics-inspired materialism has, therefore, largely taken the form of passive resistance. Muslims mostly ignore the challenges to supernatural claims implicit in the conceptual frameworks of physics. The few who respond, even today, usually just reaffirm perceptions of the universe in which supernatural events make sense. Muslims have not constructed elaborate, seemingly scientific apologetic enterprises that draw on parapsychology and quantum mysticism.

In any case, relativity and quantum mechanics have not fundamentally changed the varieties of materialism – physicalism (Brown and Ladyman 2019) – inspired by physics. Commonsense concepts of matter or causality are no longer sustainable, so that physical objects have become tied up in structures such as quantum fields. Physicists describe all events through combinations of rules and randomness, and the laws of physics are expressions of universal symmetries of nature. There is no good prospect that any signature of divine design that goes beyond rules and randomness will ever be discovered (Edis 2021a: 46–76; Edis and Boudry 2014). The nineteenth-century hope that life could be understood within physical science has largely been realized; science no longer recognizes life forces or chemical souls. Today's frontier for physicalists is to more fully understand how minds work. And our current sciences of the mind operate in a forthrightly materialist framework, expecting that solutions to our scientific puzzles will come through figuring out the vastly complex operations of human brains (Elpidorou and Dove 2018; Fields, Glazebrook, and Levin 2021).

Most critics of materialism recognize its dominance in natural science. Theologians of all religions complain about materialism and scientism (Kalın 2018; Williams and Robinson 2015); advocates of parapsychology or intelligent design creationism offer their alternatives as a way to overcome the materialism of the scientific mainstream (Dembski and Witt 2010; Tart 2009). Nonetheless, at present, most scientists judge that supernatural ideas do not present any promise of explaining anything interesting related to their particular specialty. After all, supernatural and paranormal claims have a poor track record. A kind of soft materialism reigns: no individual scientist needs to explicitly reject supernatural intervention, but the explanations the scientific community judges to be worth investigating invariably exclude supernatural agents (Boucher 2020; Boudry, Blancke, and Braeckman 2012).

This is not to say that today's science answers all the important questions. The cutting edge of science is always full of uncertainty. No one can guarantee that research in artificial intelligence and in cognitive neuroscience will wrap up all mysteries about minds, if only we wait a few more decades. Cosmology is full of knotty problems, and since physicists still don't have a good theory of quantum gravity, our understanding of physics breaks down around black holes and the big bang. No one can be ironclad certain that future physicists will not reconsider supernatural forces. But for now, the open questions in science look like they require improvements in science such as more data and better physical theories. A religious person may still hope that a supernatural agent is concealed behind scientific puzzles. But this is much like praying for supernatural intervention to help a cancer patient. The impulse is understandable, but according to current scientific knowledge, the prayer will not increase the odds of recovery.

Therefore, again, it is notable that distortions of modern physics are only a minor feature of Muslim apologetics. This is especially remarkable given the history of Muslim opposition to hints of materialism in imported science, and the strong negative reaction materialism provokes even today. Passive rejection, without investing in elaborate distortions of science, seems to work well enough.

One reason must be that, as the popularity of seeking science in the Quran demonstrates, a more-or-less traditional supernaturalist framework for understanding the universe is still a live option. The laws of physics hover in the background as a sign of divine order, while Quranic miracle stories demonstrate divine sovereignty over creation.

More important, while modern physics might motivate a form of materialism, that argument is abstract and remote. Physicalism, while a respectable philosophical position, appeals only to academic scientists and philosophers. Physics is relevant to the question of miracles and supernatural intervention. But physics does not directly touch on the concerns that most world religions address: morality, life and death, what it means to be human. With nothing quite so important at stake, most religious believers can leave descriptions of the material world to the physicists. But believers also think that where anything spiritual is concerned, wondrous exceptions happen. Supernatural forces instituted the laws of physics, and when the divine will so requires, miracles will take place.

2.3 Resisting Evolution

Biology has more to say about human life. Physics may have set the stage for emptying the universe of divine purpose, but nothing brought this loss home like Darwinian evolution. A combination of rules and randomness, acting over long stretches of time, produces the life forms we see, including ourselves.

Followers of the monotheistic religions, and even Hindus and Buddhists, have found it hard to fully accept the stark Darwinian view of life (Brown 2020). Evolution remains the most prominent example of a conflict between the content of modern science and traditional religious doctrines.

From its beginning, the Muslim encounter with evolution has been entangled with controversies over materialism. Few of the Muslims in the late nineteenth century who first commented on Darwin's theory showed much interest in biology, but some westernizers adopted the new views of evolution percolating in from Europe. The notion of the common descent of species often came wrapped up in misconceptions about a purposive unfolding of higher states of being. Since westernizers opposed the religious conservatives who they thought stood in the way of social progress, biological evolution also became part of a narrative of cosmic progress. For the conservatives, evolution was notable mainly as an example of the religious errors that were concealed in the imported foreign knowledge (Livingston 2018b; Riexinger 2011; Varisco 2018; Ziadat 1986).

Today, conservative Muslim populations continue to resist evolution. Majorities in most populous Muslim countries reject human evolution (Bell et al. 2013: 132–33; Carlisle, Hameed, and Elsdon-Baker 2019). Beyond that, however, there is considerable variation in how different countries handle science education, where evolution tends to provoke religious opposition. The Iranian theocracy has no problem accepting the common descent of non-human species. But the conservatively religious Saudi and Gulf states tend to deny all evolution, and have been the source of much crude apologetics that rejects evolution for religious reasons (Burton 2010; Determann 2015). Pakistani textbooks cover non-human evolution, but bookend all science with quotations from the Quran and praise of the creator (Ashgar, Hameed, and Farahani 2014; Ashgar, Wiles, and Alters 2010). Egypt includes evolution in the curriculum, but large numbers of both students and teachers passively reject evolution (Mansour 2011). Indonesian and Malaysian universities produce a steady stream of doctoral theses criticizing evolution. And in Turkey, suspicion of evolution combines with opposition to official secularism to produce an elaborate, actively creationist apologetics that includes pretenses to being scientific. Turkish creationism has found institutional support at all levels of education (Edis 2021b; Edis and BouJaoude 2014).

Traditional Muslim beliefs cannot easily be made compatible with human evolution. The Quran contains stories about Adam and Eve. Although Muslim theologians have not thought that the expulsion from paradise was as centrally important as in Christian doctrine, the Quran is clear that Adam and Eve were specially created and that all humans descend from them. Established interpretations of the Quran have assumed a literal Adam and Eve (Jalajel 2009). And when the Quran mentions non-human life, it does so in the context of an archaic conception of nature where divine creation is the obvious explanation for life forms.

Compared to many Christian creationists, however, Muslims are far less interested in the age of the Earth. The Quran alludes to biblical creation stories and says nothing that hints at geological deep time or the vast time scales of today's cosmology. Before modern science, Muslims accepted the common assumption that creation was a few thousand years old. But the age of the universe was never a religiously important issue, and the Quran stays vague. Therefore, Muslim creationism, even when it borrows heavily from Christian creationism, typically ignores flood geology (Yahya 1997 is an exception).

The most immediate threat that modern biology presents is that evolution is out of place in the ancient, thoroughly supernaturalist framework in which traditional beliefs make sense. Accepting evolution is difficult without treating sacred texts as religious literature that need to be suitably reinterpreted. That, however, would risk introducing a human element into revelation. For most Muslims, the Quran remains direct divine communication to which a believer must submit (Malik 2021).

Even setting aside the mismatch with scripture, many Muslims find human evolution unacceptable. As conservative Jews and Christians do, Muslims usually insist that humans are exceptional: we have an exalted status in creation, and we cannot be associated with mere animals. We are supposed to be spirits in material bodies, set in this world to be morally tested and then rewarded with heaven or punished with hell. Moreover, the social morality prescribed by traditional Islam is rooted in our created nature. Biology, therefore, is infused with morality (Edis and Bix 2005). Our religiosity and moral sense indicates an enormous gap between humans and other life forms. Evolution reduces humans to mere animals. Muslims, even when they allow that humans have a biological history, tend to argue that a separately created supernatural soul must have been infused into our material bodies (Batchelor 2017; Doko 2021).

Still, separating souls from bodies suggests some room for compromise. Like many Jews and Christians, Muslims have the option of conceiving of evolution as a divinely guided process. Darwinian evolution, as biologists understand it, produces adaptations through blind variation and selection. Many Muslims accept common descent, acknowledging that all non-human life forms are related. They insist, however, that evolution is an unfolding of intelligent design, rather than a result of variation and selection. A supernatural power directed the process to make sure that human bodies appeared, suitable for the insertion of souls (Ateş 1991; Taslaman 2007).

Guided evolution can be a popular option. It does not conflict with science as overtly as creationism, and does not interfere with secondary science education. In most Muslim countries, religious scholars have become government employees, and governments have promoted science education as part of efforts to modernize. Officially endorsed scholars, therefore, often support guided evolution. Some apologists even find hints of common descent in the Quran. And a few will claim that the idea of evolution was first invented by Muslim philosophers (Bayrakdar 1987; for criticism, see Malik 2019).

Muslim versions of guided evolution need not be committed to notions of progress in stages, the way that biological evolution has often been misunderstood among Christians. Nonetheless, guided evolution still conflicts with biology. Surveys that reveal Muslim resistance to evolution typically also show substantial minorities that affirm evolution. That can be misleading. Muslims have not been polled about evolution as thoroughly and over as long a time period as Western Christians. And the survey questions put to Muslims typically do not distinguish between guided evolution and blind Darwinian evolution. It is unlikely that many conservative Muslims fully agree with a completely scientific picture of evolution.

From a religious point of view, the pervasive randomness in modern science is not acceptable. Popular apologists, such as creationists and those who find science in the Quran, often suggest that evolution relies on pure chance to suddenly assemble structures of vast complexity. That is mistaken. And yet, apologists correctly notice that according to today's science, the history of life is sculpted by chance. Evolution includes mechanisms, such as arms races, that drive increasing complexity within lineages. Starting from the very simple, a mindless process of diversification will produce life forms that are more complex and cognitively capable. Still, evolution happens without design or foresight, as a consequence of the rules and randomness of physics. The existence of humans is a historical accident. None of this decisively rules out religious conceptions of life: as with Christians, there are Muslims who argue that divine designs manifest through natural causes in a manner undetectable by science (Malik 2021; Malik, Karamali, and Khalayleh 2022). Superficially, removing supernatural agency to a metaphysical plane restores compatibility between science and religion. But notions of invisible influences that serve a hidden purpose result in cosmic conspiracy theories (Edis 2019).

Evolution, as understood by biologists, is not a story of bodies being prepared to house spirits. Indeed, our sciences of the mind have been deeply influenced by our understanding of evolution. Variation and selection builds brains, and contributes to mechanisms within brains. One of the promising areas of research in the last few decades has been applying evolutionary perspectives on cognition and culture to more closely connect the natural and the social sciences. Such efforts are too new to have fully settled results. But cognitive and evolutionary approaches to culture even extend to explanations of religious belief. Muslims have often thought that our created nature inclines us toward perceiving the truth of Islam. Indeed, normal human minds easily acquire beliefs about supernatural agents acting on the world. This predisposition is now subject to explanations where evolution takes on a central role (Turner et al. 2017; Van Eyghen and Szocik 2021).

Conservative Muslims who resist evolution, then, have good reason to be suspicious. The materialist tendencies within modern science are corrosive of supernatural belief. And Darwinian evolution is the most dangerous conceptual framework linked to materialism. Morality, piety, religious experience – everything spiritual that religious believers think defies material explanations now attracts scientists who hope to poke and prod and examine it. The scientists usually adopt a Darwinian perspective, asking how processes of information replication and selection help explain what is happening.

Nonetheless, Muslims can still favor theological options that accept modern biology, just as they can adopt less traditional views of miracles. Theologians may promote less overt forms of divine intervention in the history of life (Malik 2021), science educators can argue that Muslims need to learn about evolution (Dajani 2015), and scientists may seek a sense of cosmic design outside of biology (Guessoum 2010).

The long-term prospects for reconciling popular religious beliefs with science through modern theologies are hard to judge. It may help, however, that most of the content of modern science has little bearing on debates concerning science and religion. No religious apologist is likely to concern themselves about the behavior of magnetic materials. Scientists of all religious persuasions can enter a lab, setting aside their cultural backgrounds when they immerse themselves in technical matters. In most scientists' careers, scientific claims and religious concerns are like ships that pass in the night, barely acknowledging one another. Religious intellectuals rarely have to address materialist aspects of science, other than an issuing an occasional denunciation. Extremely popular religious websites that answer questions from believers usually include apologetics that distort science. But the overwhelming majority of the questions they address are about details of Muslim doctrine, ritual obligations, moral concerns, and Islamic law. Believers are not overwhelmed by worries about evolution or materialism.

Nonetheless, the broad conceptual frameworks that anchor modern science are badly mismatched with traditional Islam. This does not mean that the institutions of science and religion must also conflict. If peacekeeping strategies succeed, scientists can affirm that faith has its place, and religious leaders can refrain from interfering in science education. Even so, the intellectual tension between modern science and supernatural convictions is very real. For many Muslims today, responding to that tension has come to mean misplaced claims of science in sacred texts, science denial, and even pseudoscientific enterprises such as creationism. And in the Muslim world, rejection of science is not just a feature of dissenting fundamentalist movements. Even the intellectual high culture can exhibit resistance to evolution; even institutions of higher education can harbor creationists (Edis 2021b; Livingston 2018b).

3 Clashes of Culture

3.1 Separate Spheres

Modern science challenges all supernatural beliefs. Since somewhat different doctrines may be at stake, Christian concerns about a theory such as evolution are not always identical to the worries that occupy Muslims. But fundamentally, the problems are much the same. Therefore, Muslim responses to the materialist aspects of science are often very similar to ideas explored by Christians, or, indeed, by adherents of almost any world religion. There are a limited number of options.

Popular apologetic moves such as seeking science in the Quran or embracing creationism protect religion, but at the cost of distorting science too much. Muslims are still under pressure to better assimilate modern knowledge and improve their position, even in our postcolonial times. Rejecting important conceptual frameworks of science, then, might not be the best strategy. Containing the materialist threat also requires efforts that enjoy more intellectual credibility.

In that case, one possibility is to develop modernist Muslim positions analogous to theologically liberal forms of Christianity (Masud 2009). This requires not just a softening of fundamentalist inclinations, but going against the grain of traditional beliefs. Therefore, efforts to liberalize Islam have always been contentious (Ali 2007; Kaminski 2021). Nonetheless, Muslims have the option of putting more emphasis on the human element in understanding sacred texts, reinterpreting them in order to avoid appearances of conflict with modern science (Bacik 2021).

Strategic reinterpretation, however, is not enough. Theological modernists want to recognize a proper role for science, but in doing so, they also want to establish a legitimate sphere for faith. Recognizing separate spheres for science and religion should also help dampen some of the controversies over tradition and modernity that have consumed Muslim intellectuals for centuries (Ramadan 2009).

One way to start is to observe that science and religion represent different intellectual cultures, promoting different approaches to their subjects. Western science has usually cultivated an attitude of critical detachment. Individual scientists may be hotheaded, but the scientific community as a whole must enforce a cool, disciplined skepticism. Such organized skepticism guards against common human cognitive biases and makes sure the scientific community has solid, public evidence before endorsing proposed explanations (McIntyre 2019). The culture of science separates facts from values; the demands it makes, such as not falsifying data, are narrowly focused on obtaining the facts, rather than affirming any comprehensive moral outlook.

Muslims have also made use of an ethos of scholarship. But in contrast to the culture of Western science, Muslims have historically trusted the personal testimony of pious believers. Therefore, their judgments of truth have been closely tied to Muslim conceptions of moral probity. A believer must continually struggle against selfishness, cultivate the virtues associated with piety, and aim to surrender to the divine. Indeed, a believer's capacity to obtain reliable knowledge, particularly religious knowledge, depends on their piety. Drifting away from religiously defined virtues impairs our ability to perceive the divine order in the universe. Traditional forms of Islam, finally, often demand absolute trust in the sources of religious knowledge: the sacred texts, or perhaps the Sufi master who heads a religious brotherhood (Huff 2017; Rosen 2002).

For critics of traditional Islam, the differences between the intellectual cultures associated with science and religion are another indication of a mismatch between science and traditional piety. There is a clash of cultures as well as content. Westernizers among Muslims have often described scientific practice as an impersonal application of a scientific method, celebrating the culture of science as an exemplar of openness and free investigation. In contrast, they have associated conventional religion with blind faith and obedience. The Islam of the religious scholars is supposed to be dogmatic, inflexible, slow to change – thereby impeding the rapid progress that Muslim societies require. And to go beyond importing knowledge, to *do* science, Muslims must adopt some of the more skeptical outlook that fuels modern science. Westernizers have particularly emphasized reform of education, arguing that Muslims must encourage free inquiry and open criticism, rather than the rote transmission of sanctified knowledge more characteristic of traditional Islamic societies (Demirdağ and Khalifa 2020).

In some cases, however, religion can change rapidly. Islamist ideology, for example, is a modern development, not an expression of timeless Islamic

political views. More important, encouraging skepticism in the proper circumstances need not exclude cultivating pious trust when appropriate. Theologians
can use the distinction between scientific and religious conceptions of knowledge to carve out separate spheres for science and religion.

A sophisticated defense of the sphere of monotheistic religion bases belief on
trust in a power that is overwhelming but fundamentally personal. The lived
experience of a faith opens the believer up to an ultimate reality that that
responds to religious needs and infuses purpose into existence. This purpose
goes far beyond petty individual concerns, anchoring a morality that can draw
believers out of selfishness. Responding to the divine reality encountered
through a pious life will drive a deepening trust in the sources of religious
knowledge. A believer will therefore surrender to the authority of sacred texts
such as the Quran. And all of this is perfectly legitimate. After all, we cannot
expect to approach a personal deity by maintaining a critical distance, constructing and analyzing theories, and performing controlled experiments.
Immersion in ritual, mysticism, community worship, and moral self-discipline
will be more fruitful.

Moreover, if science is defined by a scientific method, that method is bound to
have limitations. The tools that are good for physics need not work for metaphysics. Material and spiritual realities are distinct, with different ways of
knowing appropriate to each realm (Gould 1999). There are overlaps, since
the spiritual realm provides the creative spark that animates the material
universe. Therefore, a modern believer will recognize the deeper harmony
between religious and scientific knowledge, even when partisans of only one
way of knowing insist on conflict.

Variations on such theological views, which promise to give both science and
religion their due, are congenial to many Muslims. Modernizing reformers,
including westernizers, can accept a liberal settlement, as most have wanted to
preserve a distinctly Muslim culture by adopting the best aspects of modernity.
Many modern, educated Muslims, including Muslim scientists, have little
interest in fundamentalism (Ecklund et al. 2019: 125–44). They may not be as
observant as some religious overachievers, but they retain a sense of the sacred
that is rooted in Muslim tradition. If recognizing distinct spheres for scientific
and religious knowledge would prevent unproductive conflicts, almost every
Muslim should benefit.

The notion of separate spheres finds support from the way that most of the
time, science and religion barely interact, like ships passing in the night. Even
better, insulating religion from science-based criticism is intellectually respectable. Like liberal Christians, Muslim modernists can draw on currents in
philosophy that acknowledge the successes of science but insist that science

has limits. After all, how could science justify the scientific method, without arguing in a circle? Would it not be scientism, an illegitimate extension of the methods of natural science into all domains of knowledge, to dismiss other ways of knowing? Materialism may be just a form of intellectual imperialism, as morally tainted as its military relative. Muslims, therefore, can accept almost all of modern science, provided that science does not overreach and attempt to deny the divine design of the world (Guessoum 2010).

So a liberal settlement seems promising. But religious conservatives and Islamists are not convinced. There isn't much that is distinctively Islamic about a liberal modernism: it works just as well for Christianity, or almost any religion. For theological conservatives, the details are important. Islamic doctrines are not interpretive sauce poured on top of a generic religious experience. Muslims have to be correct, and the others mistaken. Almost every Muslim thinker, conservative or liberal, agrees that science has important limitations, and that in its proper place, science can be a wonderful tool. Both liberals who want to make peace with biology and conservative critics of evolution will proclaim that against materialism, nonscientific ways of knowing have to be acknowledged (Bakar 2005). But conservatives want to affirm what they think of as the true faith, not a formless spirituality. If necessary, Muslims will have to stand firm for religious truth, even when secular science appears to undermine it.

From a conservative perspective, modernists too easily let scientists have the final word. Whenever there is a real conflict in content, modernized religiosity surrenders to secular norms of knowledge production, asking only for a small protected domain of faith. For religion, this is at best a disguised retreat. Separate spheres seemingly protects both science and religion, but in practice, where serious public knowledge is concerned, liberal modernists capitulate to Western science (Toosi 2019).

Conservative Muslims are often sensitive to developments in the post-Christian West. They consider Christianity to be an inferior religion, treating its fate as a cautionary tale. The slow collapse of European Christianity does not inspire confidence. If Muslims were to behave like liberal Christians, that would invite further spread of the moral decay brought on by secular modernity (Aydın 2000). A liberal settlement may well appear plausible to rootless, atomized individuals who happen to feel spiritual. But it does little to constrain the spread of materialism in the guise of science.

To many conservatives, modernist reinterpretations of Islam look like globalized professional-class mush. Liberal modernists never make the boundaries between their separate spheres clear, leaving believers unsure about when secular science should hold sway and when a Muslim should accept religious authority instead.

3.2 A Hierarchy of Knowledge

In most Muslim countries, theologically conservative views remain an important part of the intellectual high culture. As a result, there is room for a view of
science and religion that is more robust than just claiming that science and
supernatural convictions are compatible. Muslims can refuse to adopt modern
liberalism with some Muslim sauce on top, and instead assert the primacy of
revealed truth in all intellectual endeavors (Auda 2021).

The most attractive option would be to start from a classical Muslim
conception of knowledge and update it in the light of today's conditions.
Conservative Muslims could then construct an authentically Islamic philosophy of science, as part of a broader picture that recognizes the religious ways
of knowing acknowledged by most believers (Açıkgenç 2016; Bakar 1999;
Kalın 2001; Nasr 1987).

The natural development of Islamic intellectual life was interrupted by
Western colonialism. Instead of cultivating their heritage of ideas, Muslims
were diverted into responding to the new knowledge that underwrote colonial
power. A successful response, however, could not just mean imitating Western
ways, adopting the oppressor's culture in order to survive. If Muslims were to
catch up with Western technology, becoming powerful, wealthy actors in political and economic affairs, we should then also see a Muslim civilization more
confident in its vision of scientific and religious knowledge. A more authentic
vision may indeed release Muslims from the trap of continually having to play
catch-up.

In the classical Islamic conception, there is a hierarchy of knowledge.
The religious sciences come first: they address the most foundational realities, the morally most weighty concerns (Bakar 1998; Heck 2002). And
these are not just abstract matters concerning unseen realms. Understanding
the Quran and figuring out the demands of Islamic law are critical for
successfully navigating the challenges of this life and making it into
a desirable afterlife.

Islamic civilization granted a secondary status to the foreign sciences
inherited from antiquity, recognizing their practical value. Modern science,
though vastly more powerful, can still occupy a similar place in the hierarchy.
The technological prowess generated by natural science is compelling. But
today's science, sundered from the higher truths of revealed religion, is
morally blind (Golshani 2007; Sardar 1984). Worse, science is too often
joined with a secular outlook that violates the moral order revealed by the
deeper penetration of the religious sciences.

A revived Muslim conception of knowledge will emphasize unity. Just as strict monotheism demands that everything depends on a singular divine will, a holistic Islamic vision unifies all knowledge under a single theme. If, for example, religious knowledge requires personal trust in morally acceptable sources of knowledge, that need for trust cannot be confined to a religious sphere. A scientist may think she deals with impersonal laws of nature, but that itself must ultimately be based on trust in a rational created order. Facts and values are not cut off from one another; they are unified by the supernatural purpose underlying the surface realities investigated by natural science (Hassan 2016).

Classical Muslim intellectual culture recognized the supernatural in its hierarchy of knowledge. But it did more. Incorporating the influence of Neoplatonic philosophy and mystical practices, Muslim thinkers spoke of higher realities and the ways to know them. They conceived of reason itself as akin to a mystical power of apprehending unseen realities. We moderns, with our overspecialized and fragmented intellectual lives, could benefit from such a unifying vision. A revived Muslim conception of knowledge would restore reason to its role of helping us approach the divine, rather than becoming an instrument of apostasy (Nasr 1987).

What, then, should Muslims do about the uncomfortable parts of modern science, especially those conceptual frameworks that cause trouble? Islam is not a world-denying religion; it accepts both unseen realms and the practically useful applications of true knowledge. But those aspects of modern science that cast doubt on a divine order must be due to materialist philosophical assumptions, not real science. Parts of Western science have gone astray. They will have to be Islamized – reconstructed in order to fit an overall Islamic conception of knowledge (Madani 2016; Setia 2007).

Physics might not be too difficult to handle. After all, there are still elements of mathematical Platonism in the culture of physics; some theorists insist that the laws of nature are Platonic realities and that the mathematical elegance of a theory is a sign of its truth (Tegmark 2014). The Platonism in the tradition of Islamic philosophy could enrich the Platonic relics in physics, deepening it beyond mere mathematical abstractions. A sense of cosmic order or natural cause and effect presents no problem for monotheism, as long as science can acknowledge purpose and design behind natural mechanisms.

Biology may appear more recalcitrant, as variation and selection cuts against more metaphysically essentialist conceptions of species (Dennett 2017, for qualification see Wilkins 2013). But an Islamic philosophy of science, which might include a retooled Platonism, would amend biology on a higher intellectual plane, not at the level of material details. The end result would be a revitalized, non-Darwinian biology that no longer treats intelligent design as a taboo. Instead, a properly Islamic biology would recognize divine purpose in the very foundations of its concept of life.

The social sciences should also be brought under a unifying Islamic framework. The Western versions of social science are transparently ideological, serving a liberal individualist moral agenda. A Muslim social science would accept that neutral description of social facts is a fantasy, explicitly anchoring social thought in a revealed value system. When dealing with social problems, Muslims would draw on the rich heritage of Islamic law. They would develop Islamic ideals of social organization rooted in the sacred texts and Muslim intellectual tradition, adapting them to our highly technological times (AbuSulayman 1989; Awaru et al. 2021).

Reviving classical Islamic ways of thinking is not enough: such a project risks becoming culturally insular, which may produce technological stagnation. But attempts to formulate a more Islamic vision of science can also draw on intellectual trends that enjoy global influence. Suspicions about secular Western science and defenses of nonscientific ways of knowing are common in some academic circles. Moral criticisms of the exceptionally rapacious technological civilization represented by the post-Christian West are even more common.

In the late twentieth century, many critiques of science and modernity expressed a postmodern mood. There was no such thing as scientific method. Claims to knowledge were really manifestations of power. Indeed, all truth claims proceeded from particular standpoints, which could never be neutral or objective. The standpoints of oppressed groups were, if anything, superior. The colonizing powers dismissed the knowledge systems of colonized peoples as superstitions to be swept aside by the new European science. Justice, however, demanded the rehabilitation of the ways of knowing embraced by colonized peoples (Kidd, Medina, and Pohlhaus Jr. 2017; Vaditya 2018).

Indeed, if colonialism was a crime, the contribution of Western science to this crime should also be recognized. For example, for much of its recent history, biology has been thoroughly racist. "Survival of the fittest" justified Europeans exterminating the people whose lands they stole. Genetics was motivated by eugenics (Bashford and Levine 2010; Yudell 2014). Physics has attracted massive amounts of funding by promising to build bigger bombs. Perhaps, as secular people think, facts are value-free, and science must sell its services to the highest bidder. But then, perhaps separation of fact and value is just an excuse for bad behavior. Moral revulsion at the uses of science opens up space for alternative conceptions of science that do not erase nonscientific ways of knowing and that are integrated with less predatory values.

High postmodernism had a self-devouring quality, burning up in a flash of incoherence. And rejection of all grand schemes to explain the world, treating all as a species of intellectual imperialism, does not sit well with traditional monotheism. Nonetheless, many Muslim intellectuals were attracted to postmodern critiques of Western science and modernity (Aydın 2021b). After runaway postmodern doubt did its work, faith could rebuild the world. Mere human efforts could never produce dependable knowledge. But that only highlighted the need for a divine power to underwrite all truth.

A postmodern sensibility continues to influence the humanities and social sciences today. To many scholars, moral truths and the demands of justice seem more certain than the technicalities of science. Colonized and oppressed populations have been deprived of the ability to maintain their own concepts of knowledge. When old-fashioned Western modernists accuse some communities of endorsing superstitions or pseudoscience – creationism, traditional medicine, spirit possession – they exert power to shore up a morally defective modern order. At the very least, defenders of the cognitive authority of mainstream science might be insufficiently committed to cultural diversity and inclusion (Ludwig et al. 2022; Scott 2011).

Islam has an imperial past of its own, and plenty of dead white men as heroes, even if they wear turbans. Still, as more recent victims of colonialism, Muslims can find a postcolonial intellectual climate congenial. The prospect of an authentically Muslim version of science that unites matter and spirit, fact and value, and promotes a moral approach to nature and other people can be exciting. A project of revitalizing and building on a classical Muslim hierarchy of knowledge would appear futile in an intellectual environment where secular Western forms of knowledge production enjoy an unquestioned dominance. But when Western science loses some prestige, there is more room to construct an alternative.

A renewed hierarchy of knowledge will not appeal as much to Muslims who are more at peace with modernity. Making revelation the foundation of knowledge comes uncomfortably close to affirming suspicions that Muslim intellectual cultures are characterized by their dogmatism. Ambitions to protect traditional Muslim beliefs by constructing a more Islamic science reinforce conservative habits of thought, putting further distance between Muslims and the more skeptical outlook that has led to the successes of modern science. Perhaps modernists envision a sphere for faith that is too small. But if Islamizers had their way, there would be practically no sphere for science that was not conditioned by religious doctrines.

A more Islamic science could still have been a good idea, if the world happened to work according to traditional supernatural beliefs. Presumably,

Muslims practicing such a science would then enjoy the fruits of their superior production of knowledge. But proposals to revive a classical Muslim vision of knowledge have now been in play for many decades, with no concrete achievements to show. Their results have usually been as bizarre as attempts to find science in the Quran, with an added element of hostility to Western science (Livingston 2018b: 323–32). No sciences have yet been Islamized in substance. Postcolonial complaints about Western science usually end up as sterile rhetoric that ignores the content of the science (Dasgupta 2014). Joining Islam and modern science still mostly means tacking verses from the Quran onto routine scientific work. And that is just another example of taking Western science and pouring Muslim sauce on top.

3.3 Materialism Strikes Back

Conservative and reforming Muslims argue about the proper relationship between science and religion. Much of their disagreement concerns the best way to avoid materialism. Meanwhile, while implicitly part of the debate, there are very few actual materialists around. There are some uneasy cultural Muslims who have come to doubt supernatural claims. A few openly reject the faith (Rizvi 2016), even though traditional Islam treats apostasy as a betrayal of the community punishable by death. In the days when Marxism was a live option, some public intellectuals would have expressed materialist views. Today, materialism is mostly a symbolic enemy, representing the abyss into which the religiously lax might descend if they do not right their ways. Critics of attempts to marry Islam and science almost always adopt a liberal, secularist point of view, asking the ships of science and religion to pass even further in the night (Hoodbhoy 1991).

Since the materialists among Muslims have been extreme westernizers, the materialist contribution to the science and religion debate largely derives from Western intellectual developments. And the materialist instinct is to turn science loose on itself. Science, in such a view, would not reflect a transcendent reality. Science has to be a thoroughly earthly practice, an activity of material brains, and an institution with a history and a sociology. It could well have a record of crimes as well as spectacular successes.

Academically, science studies have often been associated with a postmodern suspicion of science. Nonetheless, much of science studies looks like a scientific study of scientific practices, providing detailed accounts of institutions. Historians, philosophers, and sociologists of science examine the messy processes by which scientific communities interact with their objects of study and construct their knowledge claims.

As a result, it appears that there is no such thing as a scientific method. At least, there is no pre-set procedure that, when followed, must produce accurate knowledge about the world. Scientists use multiple, overlapping methods that seem appropriate in particular domains. Science, therefore, does not represent a single way of knowing. Modern knowledge looks like a network of descriptions linked together through relationships of mutual support, such as the positive feedback between theories and independent observations that is so compelling in physics. Methods, in such a picture, are good or bad ways of learning about the world. And whether any method is good or bad is a fact about the world, established through mutual support like any other fact of science. Methods are not transcendent principles that certify facts, and they do not require metaphysical justifications beyond earthly realities (Edis 2018a; Edis 2021a).

If all this is correct, science could possibly assimilate ways of knowing associated with supernatural beliefs, from mystical illumination to psychic insight. Our world could be such that, as a matter of fact, reading tea leaves had real predictive power. But any proposed method can fail as well as succeed. It can fail to achieve mutual support with the rest of our body of knowledge, and investigators will conclude that it is a poor way of knowing. Indeed, materialists think that religious practices are much better at producing feelings of conviction than genuine knowledge. Creationism, for example, is not wrong because approaches such as trust in scripture run afoul of a predetermined scientific method. Creationists are mistaken because accepting their claims would massively disrupt the mutually supporting networks of knowledge established by the natural sciences. And when creationism institutionalizes its practices, producing apologetics rather than real inquiry, it becomes a pseudoscience (Edis 2018b; Edis 2021a).

Just as some proposed ways of knowing do not work, so can some intellectual cultures fail to nurture genuine knowledge. It all depends on the sort of world we live in. Conservative varieties of Islam may support learning strategies that are not appropriate to our circumstances. So far, modern science has operated in many different political environments. Nationalism, for example, can encourage ethnocentric misrepresentations of reality, but it can also support scientific enterprises as sources of national prestige and power. Traditional monotheism, with its attachments to failed ways of knowing, tendencies to produce pseudosciences such as creationism, and moral strictures against religious skepticism, might not do as well (Coyne 2016; Edis 2002).

There are, however, complications. For example, creationism might be a terrible fit with the current state of natural science, but it has strong mutually supporting links with conservative moral commitments. Muslim resistance to evolution is often motivated by a conviction that nature is inscribed with a moral order. Our created nature is supposed to reflect traditional Islamic beliefs about social and sexual morality (Edis and Bix 2005). Evolution disrupts this vital moral knowledge. From a conservative Muslim standpoint, that may be a strong reason to reject evolution.

The trouble is not confined to evolution: materialist aspects of science have difficulty making room for a robust conception of moral truth. Modern forms of dissent from traditional religion are usually accompanied by strongly held moral ideals of liberal individualism and human progress (LeDrew 2016). Westernizers among Muslims often endorse a heroic image of science, taking it to represent human ingenuity when unshackled by medieval dogmas. But modern science, with its separation of facts and values and its materialist conceptual frameworks, does not endorse any universal, authoritative moral vision. The value of personal autonomy is no more closely attached to the facts of science than is religious conformity. In that case, morality may well belong to a separate sphere of knowledge. Even secularists who have little use for traditional supernaturalism might take moral knowledge to transcend mere material realities.

A materialist, however, will now turn science loose on morality. Humans, like other animals, have interests rooted in reproduction. Moreover, we are highly social animals who use our enormous brains to plot social strategies and track opportunities for cooperation and for backstabbing. Our advanced cognition and language produces channels of information reproduction separate from our genes, setting the stage for cultural evolution. We construct moral enterprises that can command our loyalties even against our biological interests.

None of the science about evolution, cognition, culture, and morality is remotely close to completion. And yet, the prospects for understanding moral perceptions and behaviors entirely within ordinary material realities are very good. Such an earthly account of morality, however, cannot entirely satisfy a moralist. Instead of universal, authoritative moral facts, a scientific explanation of morality presents us with a multitude of moral outlooks competing within a social ecology. Not every moral outlook can stably reproduce itself. But we still end up with multiple competing coalitions of interests, with an accompanying plurality of social identities and moral perceptions. We might share enough of a common human nature that most people will value conditions such as freedom or security. Such values, however, often conflict with each other and are riven with internal conflicts. And with advancing biotechnologies, human nature is not stable enough to fix what almost everyone will value. Without a transcendent realm of moral values, it is hard to sustain a unified moral vision. Instead, we end up with a moral chaos (Edis 2018a; Edis 2021a).

Such a fractured moral world is not acceptable to devout Muslims, or indeed adherents of any strong moral ideology. Moral values that transcend the material world do not help scientists explain the details of human moral lives. But belief in a transcendent morality is very useful for fortifying moral convictions, recruiting allies, and demonizing rivals. Accepting the chaos inevitably means embracing a degree of moral relativism or skepticism about morality (Blackford 2016; Marks 2013). And if an earthbound view of morality spreads through a community, this may well weaken the group's cohesion. Even if materialism about the nature of morality were scientifically correct, it would be morally unacceptable.

Intellectuals with a strong sense of morality, then, are likely to resist materialist explanations of morality. Moreover, scientific explanation is only one among many intellectual purposes. In every civilization, intellectual institutions have pursued a plurality of goals. Poking at the world and achieving accurate descriptions is one such goal, and modern science does exceptionally well at it. But historically, even more intellectual effort has been devoted to prescribing how we should live together. Institutions of higher learning have always been in the business of producing and maintaining ideology. Scholars proclaiming moral ideologies have been as socially valuable as scientists laying the groundwork for new technologies. Monotheistic religion has been particularly focused on imposing order on a moral chaos (Langermann 2012).

As a result, debates about science and religion are not intellectually resolvable. Participants have too many legitimate but incompatible goals. Materialists may insist that scientific explanations should be decisive, but religious thinkers will continue to judge claims according to a moral vision.

In the secular, post-Christian West, conflicts between different intellectual purposes do not always attract attention. The triumph of liberal individualism, and a clean institutional separation between science and religion, may make the issues seem settled. Nonetheless, ideology remains. Western liberals still go on moral crusades, make life difficult for those who do not morally conform, and even distort science when the demands of morality seem urgent. The current fervor about diversity and inclusion is an example. Liberals recognize that much about personal identity, such as gender, has to do with social role-playing. But they then let culture wars about identity put pressure on science. Moreover, they impose their new moral orthodoxy on those, such as Christian conservatives, who have a rival moral outlook. For many Western liberals today, error has no rights, and heresy is violence that does not deserve a platform (Campbell and Manning 2018). Scientists who study human sexuality and other politically sensitive subjects have to watch what they say (Abbot et al. 2023; Dreger 2015).

In the Muslim world, gender is also subject to culture wars. Conservatives who think that traditional sex roles reflect morality-infused metaphysical essences now face the demands of increasingly educated and assertive Muslim women (Dalaman 2021). Perceptions of reality, and therefore science, are inevitably entangled in such culture wars.

Traditional beliefs are still strong among Muslims: conservatives hope that an Islamized vision of science can be morally persuasive. Their rivals offer separate spheres as a sensible compromise. The goals of accurately describing the world and producing a workable ideology are not compatible. But the goal of social cohesion may still be served by sweeping such conflicts under the carpet. No doubt there will be materialists among the overeducated, who may be willing to live with moral chaos. But especially after the demise of Marxism, it is hard to anticipate that materialism will generate any potent ideology.

4 Pressures of Politics

4.1 The Westernizers Take Control

Debates about science and Islam feature scholars, scientists, and their various understandings of religion. But not every interpretation of sacred texts is influential. A televangelist may do more to shape public perceptions of science and religion than a roomful of theologians. Then again, influence can be fleeting. The most notable positions on science and Islam are institutionalized. They propagate through education. Moreover, institutions will favor some ideas more than others. If a government promotes westernization, theologians who advocate separation of science and religion will more easily find academic positions. If an Islamist style of modernization is in fashion, proposals to Islamize science will appear more plausible.

Understanding Muslim views on science and religion, then, also requires attention to how ideas are spread, reproduced, and institutionalized. Knowledge about bridge-building is rooted in experience; engineering textbooks present well-tested information about bridges that stand up. With supernatural beliefs, the constraints are less straightforward. In some historical circumstances, religious scholars have established a local consensus on the fundamentals of Islam, even as they continued to disagree about details. In the premodern Muslim empires, the scholars enjoyed a monopoly on education, which beyond a narrow stratum of elites, consisted of little beyond local boys gathering to memorize the Quran. Even today, in more conservative circles, an ideal of consensus persists.

Modernizing reforms, however, introduced new institutions, and fractured any elite consensus on Islam. Reforms started with militaries, and the training of officers, engineers, and associated medical men ushered in a European style of education. Change soon spread to imperial bureaucracies. Assimilating the new science required new educational institutions, which produced a class of officials and intellectuals with interests diverging from the religious scholars (Demirdağ and Khalifa 2020).

In the Middle East, this new professional class still served an Islamic vision of civilization, remaining loyal to an Ottoman Empire that sought legitimacy through its protection of the true faith. The new professionals proposed to manage modernization carefully, importing the technical knowledge of the West while avoiding religiously corrosive ideas. Nonetheless, the interests of the professionals were in tension with those of the religious scholars. Educated elites became a constituency favoring further westernization, even secularization, of the Empire (İhsanoğlu 2004; Somel 2001).

Many of today's controversies over science and Islam have roots in the fracturing of consensus among nineteenth-century elites. As the Ottoman state gradually collapsed, the differences between elites educated in a Western style and provincial networks of traditional scholars became sharper. Intellectuals in urban centers gravitated toward a nationalism that might appeal to the non-Arab Muslims in core Ottoman territories, most of whom spoke Turkish. The religious scholars, particularly in the provinces, remained locked into a pre-industrial economy and resented the centralizing tendencies of the modernizing Empire. They lost prestige, and the more conservative scholars resisted change, opposing what they saw as the religious deviations inherent in the new knowledge and the new institutions of learning.

Debates about science and Islam, therefore, have an important political aspect. Controversies about miracles or room for divine purpose in evolution may appear to turn on textual minutiae or metaphysical tastes, but positions about science have been closely connected to stands on state endorsement of religion or the public role of Islamic law. In environments where job security may hinge on accepting secularism, a conservatively religious academic might feel safer attacking Darwinian ideas than directly opposing a secular political order. In a conservative cultural environment, a westernizer might emphasize technical scientific matters that cast doubt on conservative beliefs.

Such controversies intensify when cultural reproduction is at stake. Westernizers typically favor a degree of secularism; they insist on separating science from religion in education. Religious scholars have lost much of their influence, but today, Islamists favor an expansive role for religious expertise in modern institutions. Islamist governments, therefore, will often provide openings for creationism in the curriculum. Political circumstances shape Muslim perceptions of science and Islam.

Political interactions between powerful institutions produce plenty of local variation, such as the way every Muslim country handles evolution in science education in a different manner (Edis and BouJaoude 2014). Moreover, institutions change. Science, with its universities and government and corporate labs, is not what it was when controversies over materialism surfaced in the nineteenth century. Islam is no longer defined by networks of traditional scholars and Sufi brotherhoods. The best approach to institutions, then, is historical: tracing how science and religion staked out their territories in a particular country, in specific circumstances.

Turkish history provides a particularly good illustration. In the early twentieth century, the new Turkish Republic, remnant of the Ottoman Empire, embarked on the most extensive program of westernization that the Muslim world has seen. Today, Turkey has also been shaped by decades of Islamist rule. During this time, Turks have confronted most questions about Islam and science and explored different institutional arrangements. The Turkish experience is not common to all Muslims. And yet, the extremes Turks have encountered, from an extensive top-down westernization to strong creationist movements, means that Turkish history finds echoes in science and religion disputes in other Muslim countries.

The leaders of the new Republic were westernizers from the military and the Ottoman bureaucracy. They proceeded to reform or abolish every institution they thought was a medieval relic. Religious conservatives interpret the two decades after the proclamation of the Turkish Republic as a calamity, where an authoritarian and aggressively secular state repressed religious expression, shut down traditional institutions of religious learning, and outlawed Sufi brotherhoods. The ruling elites saw westernization as a way of joining a universal civilization, measuring progress by the way that the wives of officials unveiled and joined their husbands in attending opera performances (Gingeras 2019).

The early Turkish Republic invested in education, including science, particularly applied science. Much of this was an extension of late Ottoman practices, such as establishing new institutions by copying European models, and sending students abroad to get a modern education. But the revolutionary period gave westernization further depth. The new republican ideals were to be made flesh by schoolteachers, who were supposed to go out into the impoverished countryside and help the peasantry into the modern age. The leaders of the Republic adapted religious language to secular purposes, proclaiming that the truest guidance in life was to be found in science. They reformed the universities established in late Ottoman times, which in the 1930s also benefited from an influx of scientists fleeing Nazi Germany. Republican policies placed all levels of education under strict state control, adopting the goal that every student should have a common education, centered on the goal of achieving modernity. Evolution became a straightforward part of the science curriculum.

While the Turkish republicans held science in high regard, their guiding ideology was nationalism. The Turkish nation had to be invented, starting with a population whose main bonds were still religious. Science, indeed, could have a role in the process. Engineering and agricultural science would improve the nation's fortunes. For some elite factions, racialist understandings of biology, common in the early twentieth century, could help define the Turkish nation by revealing its innate racial superiority (Karaömerlioğlu and Yolun 2020; Peker and Taşkın 2018).

Meanwhile, the republicans brought most religious institutions under state control. Approved scholars and religious functionaries became state employees. Religious institutions would continue to legitimate the state, but now they would have to lend support to nationalism and modernization.

Most Turkish republicans continued to think of themselves as good Muslims. But they envisioned a reformed Islam stripped of medieval superstitions and independent political power. In matters of personal conscience, basic public morality, and ritual obligations, religious institutions would still control their own sphere. But the religious scholars and the mystical brotherhoods could never again be allowed to hold back the progress of the nation. If the scholars and the Sufi masters went beyond their proper sphere, making pronouncements about miracles or presuming to dictate laws, the experience of the Ottoman collapse showed that the result would be the ruin of the Muslim nation (Alperen 2003: 100–54; Parla and Davison 2004).

The early Turkish Republic, then, endorsed a particular vision of compatibility between science and religion. Officially sanctioned theologians and scholars housed in reformed, nationalist institutions had to support modernization and science. Evolution, for example, was established science. The proper understanding of the sacred texts, therefore, had to be compatible with the common descent of life forms (Kaya 2012; Riexinger 2011). Among republican elites, the favored view about science and religion became a variety of a theologically modernist separate spheres conception. But support for separate spheres did not derive from liberal individualism and its tendency to privatize spirituality. Instead, the separation of science and religion was an imposition by the state, in service of a project of rapid modernization.

More conservative Muslim intellectuals were appalled by the secular turn of the new Republic. During the revolutionary period, many responded to the monumental betrayal by the westernizers by trying to preserve relics of traditional religious institutions, particularly in provincial areas where central government power was weak. But the most effective resistance to secular impositions came from religious movements with a modernizing character. In Turkey, the best example is the Nur movement. While remaining theologically conservative, and organizing in a form resembling a loose brotherhood, Nur adherents recognized the importance of technology, the modern professions, and education. In the early years of the Turkish Republic, however, such movements survived as persecuted underground networks (Abu-Rabi 2003; Mardin 1989).

During the peak of westernizing zeal, republicans found an opportunity to shape institutions as they preferred, carving out a space for science relatively free from religious influence. The independence of science, however, was only a minor element of the broader project of creating a secular political order. Religious thinkers continued to oppose materialism and similar skeptical views, which had real influence among republican elites (Hanioğlu 2012; Peker 2020). In the upheavals of the Turkish Revolution, conservatives found confirmation that materialism was a catastrophe for the faith. But religious resistance to secular ideology was mostly passive. Unlike in Arab countries, where scholars and intellectuals usually rejected anything associated with Darwin (Livingston 2018b), in Turkey, religious conservatives were too busy salvaging what they could from the ruins of their institutions to publicly contest ideas such as evolution.

Relationships between religious and scientific institutions, then, took shape within the broader political conflict between conservatives and westernizers, tradition and modernity. Science mattered, but conservatives had far more immediate threats to be concerned about. Creating scientific institutions was an important part of the westernizing project. But in republican education, the first priority was instilling nationalism, more than a scientific perception of the world.

4.2 Interregnum

After the Second World War, European colonial empires fell apart. The elites of newly independent Muslim countries found themselves in charge of modernization projects. They had the Turkish experience to learn from – its success as well as its excess. No other Muslim country attempted a cultural revolution as ambitious as Turkish westernization. But most adopted a measure of political secularism (Salem 1996). A viable state required modern institutions and the best technical knowledge. Science, particularly applied science, was vital for the future of the new nations.

Arab nationalism enjoyed its heyday in the mid-twentieth century, honoring Islam but also reducing the importance of religion in political affairs. The shahs of Iran opted for a top-down, authoritarian westernization. Many of the founding elites of Pakistan thought of being Muslim as akin to an ethnicity; even after the bloodbath of partition, they envisioned a more secular, rather than theocratic country. Indonesians had to forge a nation out of their archipelago, and took Islam to be just one aspect of national identity. Their post-independence politics was shaped by aspirations for a non-aligned movement and worries about communist influence, as much as by pressures from religious conservatives.

In all such cases, the military was the strongest national institution, and the state was the most plausible actor to build infrastructure and encourage economic growth. Professional elites educated in a Western style got to shape their countries after having led anti-colonial struggles. Socialist ideas, often promoted as a scientific way forward, suggested an alternative path to technological modernity that avoided the exploitative practices of the colonial West. And nationalists everywhere acted to curb the independent power of the religious scholars, often by turning them into state employees. They promoted mass education as the key to modernity and looked to applied scientists to spearhead development efforts.

None of this was unique to Muslim countries. In the nineteenth century, Russian and German intellectuals had already explored the consequences of coming late to modernity. The Japanese and Chinese had confronted the challenges of importing modern technologies and their accompanying social dislocations. Indians, achieving independence around the same time as most Muslims, wrote aspirations to promote a scientific temperament into their constitution. In the mid-twentieth century, an institutionalized separation of science and religion seemed attractive to dominant elites everywhere. Politically, the ascendance of a class of professional managers seemed foreordained; it just remained to be worked out whether their vehicle would be state-led economies or megacorporations.

Meanwhile, the Turkish Revolution had run out of steam. After the Second World War, Turkey followed a more right-wing trajectory. The ruling conservatives drew support from religious brotherhoods and the Nur movement, and strengthened institutions such as the schools set up to train religious functionaries. They brought more religion into politics, but also reconciled the largely devout population to republican institutions (Göle 2000). They adopted anti-communism, and looked toward the United States as a politically and religiously conservative power that was also at the cutting edge of technology and modernity.

Turkish elites, however, remained deeply divided. After a coup in 1960, a more secular style of westernization came back on track. The inadvertent result was an opening for the political left. Turkey continued to industrialize, experienced mass migration to urban centers, and boasted a growing and influential class of educated professionals. Significant minorities among professionals, students, and urban industrial workers were drawn toward social democratic and socialist politics. They took for granted a vision of progress led by applied science, and the strict official secularism restored after the coup allowed them to imagine that religion as a political force was limited to occasional reactionary outbursts (Landau 1974).

Passive resistance to evolution was still common in mid-century Turkey. But explicit creationism seemed confined to a small, usually provincial subculture of ultraorthodox Islam. A science enthusiast could hope that Turks would come to contribute to the grand human story of scientific progress, but the main barrier to such ambitions was economic underdevelopment. After all, Western science had entered an era of Big Science, where cutting-edge experiments required massive resources. Scientists from a still poor, still-industrializing country could only aspire to a supporting role in the international enterprise of science.

Religious conservatives continued to exert political influence, and were a leading force in anti-communist organizing. Communism, after all, seemed to be the shape that the materialist threat took at that moment. A modernity that contained an alternative to Western capitalism was attractive, but that alternative had to be found in Islam. More important, by the mid-century, the religious movements that resisted forced westernization had themselves adopted more modern forms of organization. They attracted culturally conservative, often provincially rooted students and professionals. Nascent Islamist political formations throughout the Muslim world became notable for the engineers in their leadership.

In Turkey, the Nur movement generated the most effective challenge to establishment views of science and religion. One of their rising leaders, Fethullah Gülen, denounced evolution and started to acquire more influence (Gülen 2011 [1970]). The Nur movement claimed that science and technology were found in the Quran and attacked those aspects of science, such as evolution, that were harder to force into a narrative of Quranic miracles. Nur literature of this period still bore the marks of a conservative religious subculture, but it was also becoming clear that modern media offered new ways to disseminate religious messages (Tee 2016).

In the 1970s, Islamists entered coalition governments, making evolution a minor culture war item, an indirect way of opposing official secularism. Their influence, however, was limited to symbolic victories such as inserting a disclaimer about evolution into some textbooks.

In 1980, a US-backed military coup shifted the political pressures on scientific and religious institutions. Just over a decade ago, Indonesian conservatives had solved their communist problem through mass murder. The Turkish military produced less bloodshed, but it also eradicated left-wing political options (Ozan 2012). Religious conservatives took the opportunity to promote their vision of cultural restoration – the coup era instituted a policy of "Turkish-Islamic synthesis" that rejected Darwinian evolution as a materialist error. The conservative government that eased Turkey back into civilian rule had a strong Islamist faction who ran the Ministry of Education. The Ministry sought out recommendations from creationist, Nur movement-connected academics, who then turned to American creationism for inspiration. As a result, the Ministry commissioned translations of Christian creationist literature for use in public schools (Edis 2021b).

In the post-coup Turkey of the 1980s and 1990s, official secularism entered a state of decay. Islamism not only penetrated governing institutions but, after the demise of communism, also represented the only viable radical opposition. Controversies over creation and evolution became regular culture war items covered by the mass media. Turkey took advantage of European deindustrialization and established itself as a middle-income country. Islamists, when they held power, promoted creationism and invested in religious education. The religious schools that had been operating alongside ordinary public schools had already expanded far beyond the training of religious functionaries; they now produced Islamist cadres for business and government. The Gülenist branch of the Nur movement became very influential, cultivating a "golden generation" of educated, but devout, elites intended to occupy the pinnacles of the modern professions such as the applied sciences (Özgür 2012; Weller 2022).

As it came closer to power, Islamist ideology shifted away from protest and opposition. Turkish conservatives aspired to a cultural counter-revolution, but found themselves bogged down in compromises. A modernized Islam could reign, but only if it worked together with business interests and assimilated the most up-to-date management practices. The alternative, pious, culturally authentic modernity of the Islamists fused with free market ideologies and efforts to produce a devout elite to replace the corrupt secularists (Atasoy 2009; Tuğal 2009).

Turkish debates about science and religion, then, became a feature of a culture war in an environment where all the dynamism was on the side of the Islamists. Secular intellectuals and scientists in established universities opposed creationism or notions of Islamizing science, but offered little but echoes of a discredited official secularism (Sayın and Kence 1999). An assertive new generation of religious intellectuals favored an apologetics that blended into media-driven ephemera, televangelism, and the rival religious interpretations of competing religious movements. Islamists throughout the Muslim world, however, faced a problem. They clearly were the wave of the future – an alliance between culturally conservative business leaders, professionals turning toward religious nationalism, and an urban working class abandoned by secular liberals had plenty of political potential. But ideologies have to be institutionalized. And however sclerotic, an older, more secular stratum of elites remained in charge of modern institutions. The elites had to be replaced.

4.3 A Pious Modernity

Around the turn of the millennium, Turkish creationism acquired a new look. A flood of well-produced books, magazines, and visual media products under the brand name of "Harun Yahya" appeared in the marketplace. Denouncing evolution as a blatant lie that laid the foundation of all modern evils, the Harun Yahya material portrayed an international conspiracy to undermine religion and corrupt morality.

In substance, the Harun Yahya literature was profoundly unserious: it consisted of a barely coherent assembly of complaints derived from Christian and Muslim popular apologetics. Its centerpiece was creationism, but it also strayed into messianic fantasies and conspiracy theories (Edis 2021b; Solberg 2013). Notably, however, this was creationism as a private enterprise, independent of political parties and controversies over public school curricula. And through the mass media, this creationism tried to appeal to everyone, shedding most signs of its origins in a strictly observant subculture.

The Harun Yahya enterprise was the project of a group even most religious conservatives considered to be a cult. This group was also tied to shady business dealings, corruption, and even organized crime. Nonetheless, Harun Yahya captured public attention, and through translation efforts and clever publicity stunts, acquired some influence among Muslims outside of Turkey (Lumbard and Nayed 2010; Riexinger 2009). For a while, Harun Yahya became the leading image of Islamic creationism: at home in modern media and business, coupling religious apologetics with a sense of wealth and success in the free market economy.

Entrepreneurial, media-driven creationism was flashy. But the more important recent developments in Turkey concern institutional capture. Under continuous Islamist rule since 2002, a religiously conservative vision of science and Islam became entrenched in Turkish institutions of science and science education. At the same time, Islamists put into practice the latest fashions in business, finance, and economics. The Islamists proposed to finally overcome underdevelopment: they would realize the dream of commercial wealth and military power without compromising Muslim culture (Atasoy 2009; Yankaya 2014).

In secondary science education, Islamist rule meant some mild creationism in textbooks and further expansion of the religious school system to strengthen an alternative, religion-infused system of education. In order to bring up a pious, moral generation, history would be related from a religious nationalist point of view, and science courses would downplay any hints of materialism (Eroler 2019; Yalçınoğlu 2009; Yıldız, Korkmaz, and Doğan 2019).

The Islamists also put higher education and research institutions under pressure. Efforts to produce religiously conservative cadres of experts in applied science and business-related fields had borne fruit. Gülenists, in particular, produced many of the golden generation of pious professionals who would carry out the Islamist project. The government stacked the leadership of scientific institutions with religious conservatives, often with backgrounds in applied science. They also founded many new universities, especially in the provinces. While older universities remained bastions of a secular elite with separationist views on science and Islam, in the new universities both administrative and academic personnel tended toward Islamist loyalties (Kaynar and Parlak 2005; Tekerek 2023). Turkey always had critics of evolution even among faculty in science and science education departments. During Islamist rule, rejection of evolution among the professoriate became commonplace.

The political pressure on higher education also fed back into a media-driven political environment. Unlike the post-Christian West, the intellectual high culture in Muslim-majority countries remains hospitable to conservative religious views. When a television program convenes a panel of talking heads to discuss current affairs or culture war controversies, there are plenty of Islamist credentialed experts. After all, Islamism is a mainstream view. Educated professionals, long the strongest constituency favoring westernization and a separation between science and religion, now face a challenge from an Islamist counter-elite.

Among religious intellectuals, evolution is not the only aspect of science that is suspect. Alternative medicine, for example, has enjoyed a burst of popularity. Some of this is due to media influences and westernized professionals experimenting with imported New Age notions. Many Islamist writers, however, criticize modern medicine for its materialism and neglect of spiritual realities. In any case, cultural authenticity has become a selling point in some corners of the medical marketplace. Practitioners advertise using leeches and cupping as traditional Islamic medicine, and find plenty of customers (Bulaç 2015: 115–48; Şimşek et al. 2017).

Recent events have intensified the trend toward re-Islamization. A quarrel between Gülenists and the governing party erupted in a botched 2016 coup attempt led by Gülenists (Doğan 2019). The ruling faction of Islamists responded by purging Gülenists from all institutions. Universities were severely affected; many secular academics lost their positions along with the Gülenists, often to be replaced by Islamists more loyal to the ruling party. The government then completely removed evolution from secondary school curricula, and directed an increasing share of resources to its favored religious schools. They even cracked down on the Harun Yahya enterprise and imprisoned its leaders, seeing it as a group with suspect loyalties.

Turkish creationism, meanwhile, continued to flourish. In 2017, some of the newer provincial universities started hosting annual International Creation Congresses, where over multiple days and parallel sessions, academic theologians, applied scientists, and natural scientists claimed to expose the errors of evolution and held up hope for an Islamically acceptable natural science that will uphold morality, rather than encourage nonbelief. These conferences have attracted support from among the highest ranks of religious officials in Turkey (Edis 2021b).

Such developments are not just external, politically motivated impositions on academic institutions. In contrast to Western scientists who are often drawn toward materialism, Turkish scientists, like Muslim scientists worldwide, tend to be religious believers. They need not be Islamists, and usually favor separate spheres for science and religion. But unlike their post-Christian counterparts who often perceive a conflict between science and supernatural beliefs, Muslim scientists usually affirm harmony between science and Islam – much like Indian scientists who reject the possibility of conflict between science and Hindu convictions (Ecklund et al. 2019).

Moreover, the status of science is different in Muslim countries. The need to catch up to the West in commercial and military power has promoted an emphasis on applied science. The best and brightest students go into engineering, not physics; medicine, not biology. The departments of natural science in most universities are adjuncts to the training of applied scientists. And the Islamist version of modernity fully accepts expertise in applied science as well as all practical, business-adjacent disciplines. Applied scientists tend to be more religiously and politically conservative than natural scientists (Gambetta and Hertog 2016: 128–58).

All this has resulted in intellectual environments where concerns about loyalties are never far from the surface. Apologetic and culturally defensive enterprises flourish, both among Islamist upstarts and secularists representing an older establishment. Both academic disputes and public debates keep hovering around the edges of the culture wars. Controversies about Darwin periodically flare up, mainly because creation and evolution serve as proxies for

Islamism or westernization. Few parties to the debate have been interested in biology for its own sake.

Together with such an intellectual climate, science in Muslim lands often suffers from a lack of institutional independence. Ideally, scientists should be able to pursue questions that arise from debates internal to the scientific enterprise. Due both to resource constraints and to political pressures, Muslim scientists cannot pursue such questions as frequently as they would like. Institutionalizing an internal culture of scientific inquiry has turned out to be difficult (Determann 2015, Forster 2018).

In the context of Islamist politics, the weakness of natural science need not be a concern. After all, the Islamist version of alternative modernity embraces all the useful, money-making aspects of applied science. Disputes over evolution matter only because of ideological consequences, since denying evolution rarely affects practical applications such as medicine. Islamists have bet on escaping a subordinate position in a global economy by combining proficiency at applied science with the social benefits of a unifying religious ideology (Edis 2016; Edis 2020b).

It is hard to judge whether such a gamble can succeed. Moderate Islamists in Turkey, Indonesia, and Malaysia can point to some accomplishments, but such countries have also become too mired in corruption to hold up much hope for Muslims globally. But it is also important not to judge Muslim scientific institutions by an impossible ideal of strict intellectual independence. After all, Western science, which has long represented the best practices, is also susceptible to political pressures and corrupting influences. A research scientist today spends much of her time pursuing grants while working in corporatized universities that prioritize the production of intellectual property (Mirowski 2011; Sassower 2015). And while traditional religion has weakened in post-Christian countries, ideological pressures and culture wars have not vanished.

Whatever independence scientific institutions enjoy is earned through their service to broader material and ideological interests that stand in tension with curiosity about how the world works. So far, institutions of science have not fared well under Islamist rule. But Muslims can still aspire to a pious modernity that may yet outcompete its Western rival. If any experiment has ambiguous results, as in Turkey, an Islamist can still hope to learn from the experience and try again.

5 Why Science Doesn't Matter

5.1 An Unsolvable Problem

Conservative versions of Islam, it might seem, emerge battered from their encounters with modern knowledge. If science is any guide, popular supernatural claims seem dubious, even false. Believers, especially fundamentalists, stand their ground. But they mostly produce cheap apologetics and distortions of science. There are more theological, more sophisticated ways of deflecting criticism. Still, responses that don't confront science are too often evasions, protecting religious sentiments by hollowing out their content. And grandiose dreams of reconstructing science along Islamically acceptable lines only emphasize the mismatch between cultures of piety and scientific practices of critical inquiry.

The Muslim history of grafting scientific and educational institutions onto rapidly modernizing societies also does not inspire confidence. Plenty of Muslims have joined the ranks of technical professionals vital to modern economies, including scientists. But there is almost nothing that is specifically Islamic in the work they produce. When religious and political pressures influence scientific institutions, the result is invariably a mess.

It is then tempting for reformers, especially westernizers, to declare victory in their long struggle against religious conservatives. Islam should find its proper place in the private sphere and in tight-knit faith communities, becoming an expression of personal devotion rather than a matter for public evidence and critical debate. Muslims, whatever their level of piety and observance, can and should participate in science and contribute to human progress. But religious scholars and political Islamists should not presume to dictate what are supposed to be publicly available facts.

There is, however, an alternative story. Modernizing reforms started out as prescriptions for strengthening Muslim states facing Western colonial domination. But reform was not merely a response to circumstances, still less a demand of science. Necessity turned into ideology: westernizers became enamored of not just of facts and technologies but ideals concerning social organization, political rights, and moral progress. Their opponents, the defenders of the faith, recognized the ideological aspects of the debate. While acknowledging the need to acquire the power that drove modernity, conservatives always thought they had to struggle against alien values. And at least to some extent, the conservatives succeeded. As a faith, as a set of supernatural beliefs, Islam remains strong. The more significant story, then, might be how some conservative varieties of Islam survived, even thrived, in the face of all the criticism rooted in science and modern knowledge.

Much has changed: almost all versions of Islam have become modern faiths that inhabit a modernized world. Muslims today live in cities that look much like elsewhere on the globe. They chase after dollars and cents and watch soap operas. Some chafe under dictatorships, but many periodically select between business-friendly candidates by responding to advertising campaigns. Their possessions reflect their income much more than their religion. Aside from the ultraorthodox, even their dress is distinctive mostly in the way that women usually cover their heads. Traditional modesty has long been made suitable for a consumer lifestyle by an Islamic fashion industry (Craciun 2017; Fischer 2022).

And yet, compared to the post-Christian West, Muslim supernatural beliefs and moral convictions remain alive and well. In much of Europe, organized Christianity has collapsed. Even the population of the United States, after a long lag, appears to be becoming more secular (McCaffree 2017; Schnabel and Bock 2018). Science and mass science education has contributed to the decline of Western Christianity, if only by making supernatural forces less plausible for many people. Sociologists who study European secularization, however, allow science only a minor, indirect role. Liberal individualism, material security, and the bureaucratic rationalization of everyday life are far more effective. Post-Christian consumers are not scientific materialists. They have, nonetheless, lost interest in organized religion (Bruce 2017).

Many conservative Muslim thinkers express pride that for all their troubles, their parts of the world have so far escaped that fate. The premodern networks of independent scholars have declined. But there are new sets of religious experts, new generations of the faithful eager to learn what is permitted and what is forbidden. The call to prayer still echoes in the streets, and believers still fill the mosques. Faith flourishes online (Çamdereli, Doğan, and Şener 2015). Sociologists, who used to expect that modernity would lead to secularization everywhere, today debate desecularization and point to prominent examples from the Muslim world (Berger 1999; Keskin 2011).

For conservatives who celebrate resistance to secularization, aspects of traditional Islam that draw criticism from westernizers can look like strengths. Responding to criticism by evasion or apologetic maneuvers are not virtues in a scientific setting. Philosophers of science may recognize them as immunizing strategies that protect beliefs from failure (Boudry and Braeckman 2011). But then, any ideology that coordinates belief and action at a large scale needs a healthy immune system.

If debates over science and religion concerned just the facts, Islam could long ago have become a watered-down personal spirituality and a matter of individual conscience. In a narrowly academic context, it still looks like Sufi masters cannot violate the laws of physics, or that unguided evolution best explains the data of biology. But in a world where science matters because of its practical uses, it is almost impossible to isolate views about science from political loyalties and moral concerns. And today, once the debate on science and

Islam becomes a public spectacle channeled through the mass media, it just becomes fuel to an endless culture war.

Again, westernizers, overrepresented among professionals who make a living off their expertise, may deplore the inability of science and religion to keep to their own spheres. But the boundaries are blurry. A more conservative Muslim, for example, might expect traditional morality to be reflected in the created nature of humans (Edis and Bix 2005). It does no good to simply declare that biology is separate from morality. Moreover, intellectual life always harbors purposes other than just obtaining the facts. Scientific, aesthetic, moral, commercial, or therapeutic interests are entwined together in all intellectual enterprises, and these interests regularly conflict with one another.

Sometimes multiple interests will align. In the emergency brought on by Western colonialism, importing accurate knowledge and putting applied science to work deeply mattered for all Muslim elites. But any success in defending Muslim lands, any partial westernization, also created conditions where conflicts of interest could again rise to the surface. Science, in the sense of obtaining an accurate picture of the world, is always one interest among many. In fact, science, for most participants in debates over science and Islam, has had a strictly instrumental value: Muslims had to get the practically significant facts right in order to serve deeper interests, in order to shape the world into the way it ought to be. Accuracy for its own sake might satisfy idle curiosity. But no more (Edis and Boudry 2019). Science, in other words, fundamentally does not matter.

A multiplicity of misaligned interests is a problem. Religious thinkers offer a solution. After all, the true religion is supposed to point toward the transcendent unity beyond any surface appearances of moral chaos. At the level of some inscrutable divine purpose, human interests in accuracy, morality, beauty, and happiness converge onto a harmonious whole. If a true believer is bothered by the apparent mismatch between Islam and science, she must redouble her efforts to reveal the deeper harmony.

Westernizers have usually tried to contain the moral chaos through enforcing separate spheres. But the boundaries are ever porous. The more conventionally devout eventually insist that the unseen will become manifest in the miraculous, that the divine moral order must be reflected in worldly politics. Westernizers often interpret such demands as irruptions of medieval irrationality. If so, they may even support a kind of liberal authoritarianism, where such irrationality has to be suppressed to achieve progress and liberty (Bayraklı and Hafez 2018; Bose 2018). As an ideology to harmonize interests and impose order upon chaos, liberalism is as good as any. But westernizers have also habitually equated their ideologies with science and reason. That is an overstatement at best.

If moral chaos happens to be a fact of life, then there is no resolution to debates about science and religion. There is no transcendent harmony of interests to reconcile a multiplicity of legitimate purposes. But human societies still have to cope with the disharmony. Belief systems that help societies cope will very likely incorporate useful falsehoods. After all, beliefs have costs and benefits. A rougher, more approximate description, for example, can be easier to acquire and use when compared to a more accurate model. Separate spheres may be intellectually dubious, but it can also lead to quick and clear decisions in legal contexts. Moreover, expressions of belief often signal loyalties. Sacrificing accurate knowledge may very well, on balance, be rational if it helps believers maintain religious networks of mutual aid (Edis and Boudry 2019).

They might not be literally true in a narrow academic sense, but the various mainstream views Muslims have adopted about science and religion all represent at least partial successes. It is interesting to ask whether any view of science and Islam is correct. But there is also another question: since beliefs answer to multiple conflicting interests, which approach on offer has the better prospects for cultural reproduction? It is worth speculating about the future of debates on science and Islam. Will the competition between conservatives and westernizers continue to frame the issue, or might any new approaches take the stage?

5.2 Ever More Western

Historically, westernizers have endorsed many of the science-based criticisms of traditional supernatural beliefs. Today's westernized, professional-class Muslims rarely pray at the shrines of Sufi saints, and they have almost abandoned beliefs in jinn. They may not deny the existence of angels, but they think that angelic visitations are very unusual. Proper religion keeps its focus on moral and ritual concerns, and it is pretty easygoing in what it demands in such matters. The institutions of science and religion each sustain their own sets of proper experts, who should not intrude into each other's domains.

This is an attractive pragmatism that promises to make use of both the latest scientific knowledge and the best of religious tradition. There may be different intellectual purposes to pursue, and it might not be possible to satisfy all purposes at once. But that should not prevent Muslims from adopting sensible compromises. Neither materialists who insist that science is the only reliable guide to reality, nor zealots who trace all truth to their sacred texts, will be satisfied with a liberal settlement. But there are few such people. Most Muslims have sought a middle path, pursuing worldly success as well as reassurance for an afterlife.

In practice, the constituency for the happy compromise represented by a liberal settlement between science and Islam has also remained small. The ideologically westernized part of Muslim populations rarely commands majority support. The older generation of Muslim elites who led struggles for independence and then took over the apparatus of modern Muslim states were often committed westernizers. Their descendants today still enjoy considerable power and influence – they have not been fully displaced by Islamist counter-elites. They are, however, no longer in charge.

Today's secular elites are even more thoroughly westernized. They are part of a mobile, global professional class, where a Pakistani engineer might routinely work with an Egyptian designer, together with others of diverse religions and national backgrounds. Such professionals enjoy similar educations that instill a common conventional wisdom about science and religion. Nonetheless, most Muslim countries still have distinctly subordinate roles in the global economy. Therefore, secular Muslim professionals are often caught between loyalty to the nationalisms of older generations and their present status as part of a privileged international elite, integrated with a liberal empire led by the United States.

The religion of this liberal, educated class is, unsurprisingly, eclectic. Professionals tend to favor spiritualities that are individualist and therapeutic, rather than rooted in tight-knit communities. Bookstores in Turkish cities will stock books on business success and managing stress that have an Islamic twist (Koşar 2013). But there will also be translations from Western authors who sprinkle their lifestyle advice with New Age spiritual nostrums. Astrology cycles in and out of fashion. Urban professionals may also experiment with beliefs such as karma or psychic powers. Traditional expressions of Islam, however, are associated with Islamists, or worse, a premodern peasantry. Modernized derivatives of Sufism, offering a range of levels of commitment suitable for busy consumers, are more attractive (Cengiz, Küçükural and Gür 2021).

Within secular liberal social bubbles, science has positive associations: it remains a symbol of human progress. Culturally, older generations of westernizers were often stranded between East and West. Their heirs today, now fully westernized, usually oppose claims such as creationism, mainly as a way of taking the liberal side in the culture wars.

Liberal attitudes toward Islam, however, have not spread far beyond educated professionals. And Islamists have challenged the control of education enjoyed by the older generation of westernizers. A liberal settlement certainly remains a leading, widely respected position on science and Islam. But it risks stagnation. Westernized Muslims asserting their conventional wisdom on the proper places of science and Islam may find that they persuade few people outside of their own social circles.

One possible novelty might be to reject what once seemed to be a sensible compromise. Taking science-based criticisms of supernatural beliefs more seriously, some among a new generation of westernized liberals might sever all allegiances to Islam. They might even revive materialism.

When Marxism was still a viable ideology, materialism had a noticeable constituency. Many intellectuals used Marxism, with its dubious claims to social scientific status, to give some moral depth to the purposeless universe described by the natural sciences. The religious scholars, the landlords, and the new classes of industrial capitalists and financiers represented not divine justice but bondage and exploitation. Leftist ideals of an alternative modernity and progress for the working classes, however, were continually repressed and eventually completely defeated. Marxist versions of religious doubt and materialism lost their plausibility. Notoriously, in many Muslim countries, former Marxists reemerged as Islamists, now pressing for social equality as an Islamic demand for justice. They were then defeated once again, as conservative, enthusiastically capitalist varieties of Islamism achieved power (Bardawil 2020; Tuğal 2009).

And yet, today there are some signs of renewed religious dissent. Religious doubt has been rare in Muslim societies; skepticism about all supernatural claims has been rarer still. The Muslim philosophical tradition has never generated a serious form of religious nonbelief (Akhtar 2008). Traditional Islam, with its death penalty for apostasy and insistence on community loyalty, has made dissent dangerous and doubt socially invisible. Until recently, imperfect survey data showed a level of atheism of about 1 percent or less in Muslim populations. People who describe themselves as religiously indifferent or unobservant have hovered around 15 percent in non-Arab countries such as Turkey and Indonesia and stood at less than 10 percent in most Arab countries (Schielke 2013). Lately, though the surveys are usually journalistic rather than social scientific in quality, it appears these numbers may be growing, including in notoriously conservative Arab countries (Arab World in Seven Charts 2020). Even in countries such as Turkey, where Islamists have enjoyed success, there are some signs of secularization (Ertit 2018). Alarmed commentators in popular media have expressed worries about a trend toward denial of core Muslim beliefs among noticeable numbers of young people.

It is hard to interpret all this. No doubt, some of this increased rejection of religion is due to the way that Islam has become as much a political identity as a common cultural background. Opposition to Islamist politics may well be channeled into slightly elevated levels of religious dissent. Furthermore, some among increasingly urban populations, with weaker community ties, have drifted in a more socially liberal direction. Many younger nonbelievers not only express moral disagreement with more conservative versions of Islam, they are also not satisfied with the compromises made by earlier generations of westernizers.

And then there is the internet. While televangelists and apologists have taken advantage of the new communication technologies, so have critics of traditional Islam, making counter-apologetics easily available. Muslims who question their inherited religion can now readily locate skeptical arguments online. They can find support from like-minded dissidents without compromising their anonymity. Common counter-apologetic arguments, which closely resemble the literature dissenting from Christianity, regularly draw on modern science, particularly evolution, to undermine the Muslim perception of a divinely designed universe. Some religious commentators point to perceptions of a conflict between science and Islam as a major reason for increasing doubt (Chouhoud 2016; Malik 2018).

A revival of materialism, therefore, has become possible. However, science-based criticisms of supernatural beliefs are only part of the newly visible arguments against Islam. Dissent appears driven largely by moral discomfort with traditional practices and Islamist politics. Even when arguments against religion have more substance, they tend to raise ancient metaphysical conundrums. For example, unlike Christianity, the problem of reconciling suffering with a divinely created universe has not been prominent in the Islamic philosophical and theological tradition. Today, there is renewed popular interest in whether the evils of the world are compatible with divine purpose (Edis 2021c). None of this, however, requires much interest in science. Nonbelievers who grapple with the way that materialism tends to make all comprehensive moral frameworks insecure are even rarer.

It is therefore very difficult to predict how the current forms of religious dissent might affect long-standing debates about science and Islam. Nonbelief has become more visible, but it is still confined to a small minority, and it is largely reactive in nature. The Marxist materialists of old had ambitions to draw in the working class. They were mistaken in their expectations: suspicions of religious deviance always undercut support for leftist politics among Muslims. Today's expressions of religious dissent are much more individualist and identitarian in character. Therefore, they are likely to be politically inconsequential, except as an ingredient for more culture wars.

Nonbelief among cultural Muslims appears to be largely a form of ultraliberal moral conviction, rather than a stance inspired directly by modern science. And right now, all versions of liberal Islam are caught up in the present crisis of

Muslim secularism. The post-independence secular regimes in Muslim countries have failed to develop much appeal beyond the more westernized factions of educated professionals. Varieties of secular liberal views of science and religion, whether separate spheres or some kind of science-inspired materialism, depend on the political fortunes of the professional class and the modern state. Nothing about that situation has fundamentally changed.

In the more medium-term future, a more serious problem is the prospect of environmental catastrophe (Bradshaw et al. 2021). Westernized Muslims are invested in the fortunes of political liberalism, from its ideals of progress to its international imperial order. Since the impetus for westernization was catching up to Western technology and power, a mindset of growth and development at all costs prevails. Environmental interests are largely boutique lifestyle concerns.

Muslim critics of amoral Western science often point to environmental degradation as a consequence of the exploitative nature of Western science (Saniotis 2012; Sardar 2006: 91–107). Such criticism is opportunistic – the recent Islamist environmental record has been typical of capitalist development everywhere. Nonetheless, the practical problem our environmental predicament poses for liberals remains. Without steady economic growth, without the consumerist forms of progress, much of the plausibility of a liberal settlement will vanish.

Westernizers have been driven by the long emergency of having to catch up to the industrialized colonial powers. They have had little opportunity to reflect on whether ever-intensifying extractive development was a good idea. Environmental crises such as climate change are likely to leave westernized Muslims with fewer rationales for their culture war positions. As circumstances change, the older compromises will not be as practical anymore.

5.3 A Useful Mess

From the start, Muslim debates about science and religion have been closely linked to the question of how much of Islamic civilization had to be sacrificed in order to assimilate the new knowledge. Conservatives wanted to keep westernization to a minimum. At the beginning of the debates, it was not clear exactly what this minimum was. Today, after more than two centuries of modernization efforts, perhaps it is easier to decide where to draw the line.

The westernizers have been correct that traditional Muslim cultures presented too many obstacles for science and technology. Even so, some very traditional forms of faith remain attractive. The older, hierarchical concept of knowledge, often linked to mystical practices and an otherworldly orientation, may seem just the antidote to modern disillusionment. A more traditional approach promises a unified picture of reality that answers to the deepest aspirations of believers, integrated with a way of life that demands piety and self-discipline.

Religious brotherhoods still offer such a way of life (Raudvere and Stenberg 2009). There are practical advantages as well: in a modern economy, brotherhoods can provide a form of solidarity that competes with meritocratic individualism. To professional-class liberals, such solidarity appears as a form of corruption. Nonetheless, brotherhoods do not just provide material advantages – piety holds everything together. Believers can find a conviction of profound truths, moral enlightenment, and personal contentment. The problem remains, however, that thoroughly supernatural conceptions of reality are at odds with modern science. They are technologically sterile.

The most insistently Islamic ways of life, then, are likely to be confined to communities of religious overachievers. Such enclaves of piety usually rely on a wider circle of more worldly believers, including businessmen and professionals, to support their enterprise. As long as there are enough who can take care of the technical aspects of modern life, enclaves can flourish.

Such focused communities are not a historical novelty. Ordinary Muslims have most often been on the outskirts of communities of intense devotion, not in their inner circle. But today, maintaining a way of life that supports traditional concepts of knowledge is more complicated. Classical Islamic civilization is irretrievably lost. Muslims no longer live in environments where supernatural perceptions of the universe are virtually unchallenged. There still are plenty of religious experts, often academics, who defend a traditional ideal. But to outsiders, their efforts look like exercises in intellectual nostalgia. In any case, today, Muslims who are disturbed by a mismatch between science and religion have other options.

The main competition to traditionalists comes from those who might be broadly called Islamists. Islamism often appears to be an ideology with little concern about science and theology, beyond its tendency toward fundamentalism. Politically, however, even when not in power, Islamists have captured the imagination of Muslims worldwide. Mainstream conservatives and religious nationalists everywhere have come to reflect something of the Islamist attitudes toward modernity. And moderate, business-friendly Islamism has stumbled onto its own ideas about what to take from the West and what to reject (Edis 2016).

The moderate Islamist position on science is hard to pin down. Compared to traditionalists, Islamists are less concerned with a unified religious vision. In fact, views on science that travel together with political Islam are something of a jumble. We have creationism, prophetic medicine, cheap miracles – a motley collection of apologetic strategies and pseudosciences that are shaped by a competition for media attention as much as any roots in Muslim tradition. The vision of a science harmonious with Islam, shaped by devout applied scientists and entrepreneurs of belief, is most often populist, opportunist, even superficial in character. A sympathetic observer might call this vision eclectic; a more severe critic would consider it incoherent. It is a bit of a mess.

The moderate Islamist option also accepts a vast amount of westernization. For example, Muslims everywhere have largely adopted modern financial institutions, including banking and corporations, even though they are not recognized in traditional Islamic law. The sacred texts frown on charging interest, but no Muslim faction with credible claims to running a modern economy can avoid it. Therefore, some very conservative Muslims have engaged in all the creative reinterpretation and rule-bending necessary to make this happen (Kuran 2004; Kuran 2011). Islamist ideology would not be conceivable without considerable prior westernization. Some scholars even argue that in a backhanded way, Islamism has been a secularizing force in Muslim societies (Iqtidar 2011; Kazemipur 2022).

One problem with such extensive adoption of modern ways is that claims of cultural authenticity start ringing hollow – the illusion of authenticity comes from pouring Muslim sauce over Western substance. Some will wear European dress and add a headscarf, others will embrace electrical engineering and promote creationism.

There is, however, a pattern behind the Western ways embraced by conservatives. Modern economies have meant not just new technologies but new forms of social organization that affect even the roles of the sexes and the structure of families. Here, Western countries have tended toward a liberal individualism suspicious of all unchosen encumbrances, including faith and family. Most Muslims have responded differently. Moderate Islamists have been very effective in politically mobilizing conservative women, and have promoted a more conservative ideal for the sexes. Women, in their view, must be modest and pious but can still be publicly active and engaged in the professions. This is very different from a more rigidly traditional ideal that tends to seclude women in the private family compound.

So the headscarf may not be so superficial after all. Conservative Muslims hope to modernize in a way that protects family ties and sex roles. Islamic feminists try to reinterpret sacred texts to further the interests of women, criticizing how religious expertise has usually been monopolized by men. But most Muslim feminists are not interested in promoting a liberal conception of individual autonomy above all. They remain committed to faith, family, and the complementarity of the sexes. While modern Muslims experiment with new arrangements to meet today's economic demands, they also resist Western ideologies that corrode a more Muslim way of life (Edis 2016: 133–66; Mahmood 2001).

Conservative Muslim approaches to science are similar. Science is useful. Technology is vital. Nonetheless, science does not matter enough to put central supernatural convictions at risk. In that case, what outsiders might perceive as eclecticism or incoherence is perhaps better understood as a willingness to experiment. Muslims who do not retreat into pious enclaves also have to immunize their beliefs from challenges, often by wrapping important beliefs in protective layers of pseudoscience. The result looks like a mess, since what works to protect core beliefs is not always obvious, and can change with time and circumstances. Discovering what works requires experimentation.

In time, if industrial civilization avoids self-destruction, even the Muslim sauce poured on top of modern practices might transform what it covers. What starts out as fake science might evolve into more sophisticated theological means of evading criticism. For now, however, we should still expect something of a mess.

In any case, it is not just conservative Muslims who find themselves pulled in many different directions. I have to confess to some of that myself. By temperament and by training, I am a physics chauvinist. My sympathies, therefore, are with materialism. I grew up in a social bubble dominated by westernizers; embracing Western ways comes naturally to me. But my views are not popular among Muslims, and so I sometimes have to resort to stereotypical separate spheres rhetoric, even though it has serious intellectual flaws.

A few years ago, in an introductory physics class, I started discussing quantum mechanics, pointing out how it presents us with a microscopic world that operates randomly. One of my students then blurted out a question: but then, what about God? In the American Midwestern university where I teach, most students are Christian or secular. This student was Muslim. And she recognized, perhaps, the difficulty that randomness poses when the world was supposed to be a product of divine design.

At first, it seemed that this was a great question. Here was a student really paying attention, not passively filing what I said into a box labeled "for the physics exam" but recognizing connections with her other interests. I could even have interpreted the question as an invitation to mount one of my favorite hobbyhorses.

But then again, I wanted my students to learn physics. If my questioner felt her religion challenged, she could become less enthusiastic about science. I don't want to help produce more creationists. And any amount of time

I spent exploring the question would be less time for me to help all my students understand some very tricky physics to follow.

So I didn't take any risks. I said that the issue was interesting, but physicists tended not to talk about religion. There were a few Christian and Muslim theologians who addressed the question, and I would be happy to suggest some books to anyone who would ask later. I did not mention that I was not impressed with such theological efforts. And then I moved on to a calculation that was relevant for the coming exam.

For anyone who has an overwhelming interest in satisfying their curiosity, science will matter a lot. For the rest of us, even in the science classroom, there are many competing interests to balance, and we may find ourselves in a bit of a mess. For most Muslims today, well satisfied with their faith and caught up in the practical problems of modern life, science does not matter very much.

References

Abbot, D., Bikfalvi, A., Bleske-Rechek, A. et al. (2023). In defense of merit in science. *Journal of Controversial Ideas*, 3(1), 1.

Abu-Rabi, I. M., ed. (2003). *Islam at the Crossroads: On the Life and Thought of Bediuzzaman Said Nursi*. Albany: State University of New York Press.

AbuSulayman, A., ed. (1989). *Islamization of Knowledge: General Principles and Work Plan*, 2d ed. Herndon: International Institute of Islamic Thought.

Açıkgenç, A. (2016). Philosophy of science in epistemological perspective. In M. H. Kamali, O. Bakar, D. A. Batchelor, & R. Hashim, eds., *Islamic Perspectives on Science and Technology: Selected Conference Papers*. Singapore: Springer, pp. 59–74.

Akhtar, S. (2008). *The Quran and the Secular Mind: A Philosophy of Islam*. New York: Routledge.

Akhtar, S. (2018). The performance of Islamic countries' financial and economic systems since the 1990s. In Ö. Ü. Eriş, & A. S. İkiz, eds., *The Political Economy of Muslim Countries*, Newcastle: Cambridge Scholars, pp. 35–63.

Akhter, S. (2009). *Faith and Philosophy of Islam*. Delhi: Kalpaz Publications.

Aksa, F. I. (2020). Islamic perspectives in disaster: An alternative to changing fatalistic attitudes. *Jamba*, 12(1), 942.

Al-Hassani, S. T. S., Woodcock, E., & Saoud, R., eds. (2012). *1001 Inventions: Muslim Heritage in Our World*, Manchester: Foundation for Science, Technology and Civilisation.

Ali, M. M. (2007). Liberal Islam: an analysis. *American Journal of Islamic Social Sciences*, 24(2), 44–70.

Alperen, A. (2003). *Sosyolojik Açıdan Türkiye'de İslam ve Modernleşme: Çağımız İslam Dünyasında Modernleşme Hareketleri ve Türkiye'deki Etkileri*. Adana: Karahan Kitabevi.

The Arab World in Seven Charts: Are Arabs Turning Their Backs on Religion? (2019). *BBC News* (June 24), www.bbc.com/news/world-middle-east-48703377 (accessed October 9, 2022).

Ashgar, A., Hameed, S., & Farahani, N. K. (2014). Evolution in biology textbooks: a comparative analysis of 5 Muslim countries. *Religion and Education*, 41(1), 1–15.

Asghar, A., Wiles, J. R., & Alters, B. (2010). The origin and evolution of life in Pakistani high school biology. *Journal of Biological Education*, 44(2), 65–71.

Atasoy, Y. (2009). *Islam's Marriage with Neoliberalism: State Transformation in Turkey*. New York: Palgrave McMillan.

Ateş, S. (1991). *Gerçek Din Bu*, vol. 1. İstanbul: Yeni Ufuklar Neşriyat.

Auda, J. (2021). *Re-envisioning Islamic Scholarship: Maqasid Methodology as a New Approach*. Milpitas: Claritas Books.

Awaru, A. O. T., Salam, R., Torro, S., & Suhaeb, F. W. (2021). The Islamization of the social sciences: A review. *GNOSI*, 4(3), 24–41.

Aydın, H. (2021a). *İslam Kültüründe Felsefenin Krizi ve Aydınlanma Sorunu*. Bursa: Sentez Yayıncılık.

Aydın, H. (2021b). *Eleştirel Aklın Işığında Postmodernizm ve Yansımaları*. Bursa: Sentez Yayıncılık.

Aydın, M. S. (2000). *İslâm'ın Evrenselliği*. İstanbul: Ufuk Kitapları.

Aysan, A. F., Babacan, M., Gur, N., & Karahan, H., eds. (2018). *Turkish Economy: Between Middle Income Trap and High Income Status*. Cham: Palgrave Macmillan.

Bacik, G. (2021). *Contemporary Rationalist Islam in Turkey: The Religious Opposition to Sunni Revival*. London: I. B. Tauris.

Bakar, O. (1998). *Classification of Knowledge in Islam: A Study in Islamic Philosophies of Science*. Cambridge: Islamic Texts Society.

Bakar, O. (1999). *The History and Philosophy of Islamic Science*. Cambridge: Islamic Texts Society.

Bakar, O. (2005). Gülen on religion and science: A theological perspective. *The Muslim World* 95(3), 359–72.

Bardawil, F. A. (2020). *Revolution and Disenchantment: Arab Marxism and the Binds of Emancipation*. Durham: Duke University Press.

Bashford, A., & Levine, P., eds. (2010). *The Oxford Handbook of the History of Eugenics*. New York: Oxford University Press.

Batchelor, D. A. (2017). Adam and Eve's origin: A theory harmonising scientific evidence with the Qur'anic text. *Theology and Science*, 15(4), 490–508.

Bayrakdar, M. (1987). *İslam'da Evrimci Yaradılış Teorisi*. İstanbul: İnsan Yayınları.

Bayraklı, E., & Hafez, F., eds. (2018). *Islamophobia in Muslim Majority Societies*. London: Routledge.

Bell, J., Lugo, L., Cooperman, A. et al. (2013). *The World's Muslims: Religion, Politics and Society*. Washington: Pew Research Center.

Berger, P. L., ed. (1999). *The Desecularization of the World: Resurgent Religion and World Politics*. Grand Rapids: William B. Eerdmans.

Berkes, N. (1998). *The Development of Secularism in Turkey*. New York: Routledge.

Bigliardi, S. (2011). Snakes from staves? science, scriptures and the supernatural in Maurice Bucaille. *Zygon*, 46, 793–805.

Bigliardi, S. (2014). The contemporary debate on the harmony between Islam and science: Emergence and challenges of a new generation. *Social Epistemology*, 28(2), 167–86.

Bigliardi, S. (2017). The "scientific miracle of the Qur'ān," pseudoscience, and conspiracism. *Zygon* 52(1), 146–71.

Blackford, R. (2016). *The Mystery of Moral Authority*. New York: Palgrave Macmillan.

Blake, S. P. (2016). *Astronomy and Astrology in the Islamic World*. Edinburgh: Edinburgh University Press.

Bose, S. (2018). *Secular States, Religious Politics: India, Turkey, and the Future of Secularism*. Cambridge: Cambridge University Press.

Boucher, S. C. (2020). Methodological naturalism in the sciences. *International Journal for Philosophy of Religion*, 88, 57–80.

Boudry, M., Blancke, S., & Braeckman, J. (2012). Grist to the mill of anti-evolutionism: the failed strategy of ruling the supernatural out of science by philosophical fiat. *Science & Education*, 21, 1151–65.

Boudry, M., & Braeckman, J. (2011). Immunizing strategies and epistemic defense mechanisms. *Philosophia*, 39, 145–61.

Bradshaw, C. J. A., Ehrlich, P. R., Beattie, A., et al. (2021). Underestimating the challenges of avoiding a ghastly future. *Frontiers in Conservation Science*, 1, 615419.

Brentjes, S., Edis, T., & Richter-Bernburg, L., eds. (2016). *1001 Distortions: How (Not) to Narrate History of Science, Medicine, and Technology in Non-Western Cultures*. Würtzburg: Ergon-Verlag.

Brown, C. M., ed. (2020). *Asian Religious Responses to Darwinism: Evolutionary Theories in Middle Eastern, South Asian and East Asian Cultural Contexts*. Dordrecht: Springer.

Brown, R. G., & Ladyman, J. (2019). *Materialism: A Historical and Philosophical Inquiry*. London: Routledge.

Bruce, S. (2008). *Fundamentalism*. Cambridge: Polity Press.

Bruce, S. (2017). *Secular Beats Spiritual: The Westernization of the Easternization of the West*. New York: Oxford University Press.

Bulaç, A. (2015). *İnsanın Özgürlük Arayışı*. İstanbul: İnkılap Kitabevi.

Bulğen, M. (2019). The criticism of materialism in late Ottoman's new science of kalām, *ULUM*, 2(1), 133–67.

Burçak, B. (2008). Modernization, science and engineering in the early nineteenth century Ottoman Empire. *Middle Eastern Studies*, 44(1), 69–83.

Burton, E. K. (2010). Teaching evolution in Muslim states: Iran and Saudi Arabia compared. *Reports of the National Center for Science Education*, 30(3), 28–32.

Çalışkan, M. T., ed. (2020). *Kur'an ve Pozitif Bilim*. İstanbul: KURAMER Yayınları.

Çamdereli, M., Doğan, B. Ö., & Şener, N. K., eds. (2015). *Dijitalleşen Din*. İstanbul: Köprü Kitapları.

Campbell, B., & Manning, J. (2018). *The Rise of Victimhood Culture: Microaggressions, Safe Spaces, and the New Culture Wars*. Cham: Palgrave Macmillan.

Carlisle, J., Hameed, S., & Elsdon-Baker, F. (2019). Muslim perceptions of biological evolution: A critical review of quantitative and qualitative research. In S. H. Jones, R. Catto, & T. Kaden, eds., *Science, Belief and Society: International Perspectives on Religion, Non-Religion and the Public Understanding of Science*. Bristol: Bristol University Press, pp. 147–170.

Cengiz, K., Küçükural, Ö., & Gür, H. (2021). *Türkiye'de Spiritüel Arayışlar Deizm, Yoga, Budizm, Meditasyon, Reiki vb*. İstanbul: İletişim Yayınları.

Chester, D. K., Duncan, A. M., & Al Ghasyah Dhanhani, H. (2013). Volcanic eruptions, earthquakes and Islam. *Disaster Prevention and Management*, 22(3), 278–92.

Chouhoud, Y. (2016). Modern pathways to doubt in Islam. *Yaqeen Institute for Islamic Research*, https://yaqeeninstitute.org/youssef-chouhoud/modern-pathways-to-doubt-in-islam (accessed October 9, 2022).

Coyne, J. A. (2016). *Faith Versus Fact: Why Science and Religion Are Incompatible*. New York: Penguin Books.

Craciun, M. (2017). *Islam, Faith, and Fashion: The Islamic Fashion Industry in Turkey*. London: Bloomsbury.

Dajani, R. (2015). Why I teach evolution to Muslim students. *Nature*, 520, 409.

Dalaman, Z. B. (2021). From secular Muslim feminism to Islamic feminism(s) and new generation Islamic feminists in Egypt, Iran and Turkey. *Border Crossing*, 11(1), 77–91.

Dallal, A. S. (2010). *Islam, Science, and the Challenge of History*. New Haven: Yale University Press.

Dasgupta, S. (2014). Science studies "sans" science: Two cautionary postcolonial tales. *Social Scientist*, 42(5/6), 43–61.

Dembski, W. A., & Witt, J. (2010). *Intelligent Design Uncensored: An Easy-to-Understand Guide to the Controversy*. Downers Grove: InterVarsity Press.

Demirdağ, S., & Khalifa, M. (2020). The effects of westernization efforts on the Turkish education system. *International Journal of Educational Research Review*, 5(3), 165–77.

Dennett, D. C. (2017). Darwin and the overdue demise of essentialism. In D. L. Smith, ed., *How Biology Shapes Philosophy: New Foundations for Naturalism*. Cambridge: Cambridge University Press, pp. 9–22.

Determann, J. M. (2015). *Researching Biology and Evolution in the Gulf States: Networks of Science in the Middle East*. London: I. B. Tauris.

Doğan, R. (2019). *Political Islamists in Turkey and the Gülen Movement*. Cham: Palgrave Macmillan.

Doko, E. (2021). Islam and evolution: A defense. *Kader*, 19(3), 899–913.

Dreger, A. (2015). *Galileo's Middle Finger: Heretics, Activists, and the Search for Justice in Science*. New York: Penguin.

Ecklund E. H., Johnson, D. R, Vaidyanathan, B. et al. (2019). *Secularity and Science: What Scientists around the World Really Think about Religion*. New York: Oxford University Press.

Edis, T., & Bix, A. S. (2005). Biology and "created nature": Gender and the body in popular Islamic literature from modern Turkey and the West. *Arab Studies Journal*, 12(2)/13(1), 140–58.

Edis, T. (2002). *The Ghost in the Universe: God in Light of Modern Science*. Amherst: Prometheus Books.

Edis, T. (2007). *An Illusion of Harmony: Science and Religion in Islam*. Amherst: Prometheus Books.

Edis, T. (2008). *Science and Nonbelief*. Amherst: Prometheus Books.

Edis, T. (2009). Muslim resistance to Darwinian evolution. In J. Seckbach, & R. Gordon, eds., *Divine Action and Natural Selection: Science, Faith and Evolution*. Singapore: World Scientific, pp. 519–32.

Edis, T. (2016). *Islam Evolving: Radicalism, Reformation, and the Uneasy Relationship with the Secular West*. Amherst: Prometheus Books.

Edis, T. (2018a). Two cheers for scientism. In M. Boudry, & M. Pigliucci, eds., *Science Unlimited? The Challenges of Scientism*. Chicago: University of Chicago Press, pp. 73–94.

Edis, T. (2018b). From creationism to economics: how far should analyses of pseudoscience extend? *Mètode Science Studies Journal*, 8, 141–47.

Edis, T. (2019). Cosmic conspiracy theories: how theologies evade science. In J. Seckbach, & R. Gordon, eds., *Theology and Science: From Genesis to Astrobiology*. Singapore: World Scientific, pp. 143–66.

Edis, T. (2020a). A revolt against expertise: pseudoscience, right-wing populism, and post-truth politics. *Disputatio Philosophical Research Bulletin*, 9(13), 67–95.

Edis, T. (2020b). The politics of Islamic opposition to evolution in Turkey. In C. M. Brown, ed., *Asian Religious Responses to Darwinism: Evolutionary Theories in Middle Eastern, South Asian, and East Asian Cultural Contexts*. Cham: Springer, pp. 19–36.

Edis, T. (2021a). *Weirdness!: What Fake Science and the Paranormal Tell Us About the Nature of Science.* Durham: Pitchstone.

Edis, T. (2021b). The Turkish model of Islamic creationism. *Almagest*, 12, 40–65.

Edis, T. (2021c). Doubt and submission: why evil is a minor problem for Islam. In J. W. Loftus, ed., *God and Horrendous Suffering.* Denver: GCRR Press, pp. 304–25.

Edis, T., & Bix, A. S. (2016). Flights of fancy: The "1001 inventions" exhibition and popular misrepresentations of medieval Muslim science and technology. In S. Brentjes, T. Edis, & L. Richter-Bernburg, eds., *1001 Distortions: How (Not) to Narrate History of Science, Medicine, and Technology in Non-Western Cultures.* Würtzburg: Ergon-Verlag, pp. 189–200.

Edis, T., & Boudry, M. (2014). Beyond physics? on the prospects of finding a meaningful oracle. *Foundations of Science*, 19(4), 403–22.

Edis, T., & Boudry, M. (2019). Truth and consequences: When is it rational to accept falsehoods? *Journal of Cognition and Culture*, 19, 153–75.

Edis, T., & BouJaoude, S. (2014). Rejecting materialism: Responses to modern science in the Muslim Middle East. In M. R. Matthews, ed., *International Handbook of Research in History, Philosophy and Science Teaching* Volume III. Dordrecht: Springer, pp. 1663–90.

Elpidorou, A., & Dove, G. (2018) *Consciousness and Physicalism: A Defense of a Research Program.* New York: Routledge.

Elsakaan, N., & Longo, M. (2016). The embryo development in Quranic verses. *Medicina Nei Secoli Arte e Scienza*, 28(3), 921–38.

Elshakry, M. (2020). The invention of the Muslim Golden Age: universal history, the Arabs, science, and Islam. In D. Edelstein, N. Wheatley, & S. Geroulanos, eds., *Power and Time: Temporalities in Conflict and the Making of History.* Chicago: University of Chicago Press, pp. 80–102.

El-Zein, A. (2009). *Islam, Arabs, and the Intelligent World of the Jinn.* Syracuse: Syracuse University Press.

Eroler, E. G. (2019). *"Dindar Nesil Yetiştirmek": Türkiye'nin Eğitim Politikalarında Ulus ve Vatandaş İnşası (2002–2016).* İstanbul: İletişim Yayıncılık.

Ertit, V. (2018). God is dying in Turkey as well: application of secularization theory to a non-Christian Society. *Open Theology*, 4(1), 192–211.

Fard, R. M. N., Moslemy M., & Golshahi, H. (2013). The history of modern biotechnology in Iran: a medical review. *Journal of Biotechnology and Biomaterials*, 3(2), 1000159.

Fields, C., Glazebrook, J. F., & Levin, M. (2021). Minimal physicalism as a scale-free substrate for cognition and consciousness. *Neuroscience of Consciousness*, 7(2), niab013.

Fischer, J. (2022). Muslim material culture: Western perspectives and global markets. In R. Tottoli, ed., *Routledge Handbook of Islam in the West*, 2nd ed. New York: Routledge, pp. 348–62.

Forster, N. (2018). Why are there so few world-class universities in the Middle East and North Africa? *Journal of Further and Higher Education*, 42(8), 1025–39.

Gambetta, D., & Hertog, S. (2016). *Engineers of Jihad: The Curious Connection between Violent Extremism and Education*. Princeton: Princeton University Press.

Geraci, R. M. (2018). *Temples of Modernity: Nationalism, Hinduism, and Transhumanism in South Indian Science*. Lanham: Lexington Books.

Gingeras, R. (2019). *Eternal Dawn: Turkey in the Age of Atatürk*. New York: Oxford University Press.

Göle, N. (2000). *İslam ve Modernlik Üzerine Melez Desenler*. İstanbul: Metis Yayınları.

Golshani, M. (2007). Science for humanity: An Islamic perspective. *Islam & Science*, 5(2), 179–90.

Gould, S. J. (1999). *Rocks of Ages: Science and Religion in the Fullness of Life*. New York: Ballantine.

Gregory, F. (1977). *Scientific Materialism in Nineteenth Century Germany*. Dordrecht: Springer.

Guénon, M. (2019). ʿAbd al-Majīd al-Zindānī's iʿjāz ʿilmī approach: embryonic development in Q. 23:12–14 as a scientific miracle. *Journal of Qurʾanic Studies*, 21(3), 32–56.

Guessoum, N. (2010). *Islam's Quantum Question: Reconciling Muslim Tradition and Modern Science*. London: Bloomsbury.

Guessoum, N., & Osama, A. (2015a). Institutions: revive universities of the Muslim world. Nature, 526, 634 -36.

Guessoum, N., & Osama, A., eds. (2015b). *Report of Zakri Task Force on Science at Universities of the Muslim World*. Islamabad: Muslim World Science Initiative.

Gülen, M. F. (2011). *Yaratılış Gerçeği ve Evrim*. İstanbul: Nil Yayınları.

Hanioğlu, M. Ş. (2008). *A Brief History of the Late Ottoman Empire*. Princeton: Princeton University Press.

Hanioğlu, M. Ş. (2012). The historical roots of Kemalism. In A. T. Kuru, & A. C. Stepan, eds., *Democracy, Islam, and Secularism in Turkey*. New York: Columbia University Press, pp. 32–60.

Haq, I. U., & Tanveer, M. (2020). Status of research productivity and higher education in the members of the Organization of Islamic Cooperation (OIC). *Library Philosophy and Practice (e- Journal)*, 3845.

Hassan, L. (2020). *Ash 'arism Encounters Avicennism: Sayf al-Dīn al-Āmidī on Creation*. Piscataway: Gorgias Press.

Hassan, M. K. (2016). The necessity of studying the natural sciences from the Qur'anic worldview. In M. H. Kamali, O. Bakar, D. A. Batchelor, & R. Hashim, eds., *Islamic Perspectives on Science and Technology: Selected Conference Papers*. Singapore: Springer, pp. 35–58.

Heck, P. (2002). The hierarchy of knowledge in Islamic civilization. *Arabica*, 49(1), 27–54.

Hoodbhoy, P. (1991). *Islam and Science: Religious Orthodoxy and the Battle for Rationality*. London: Zed Books.

Hill, H., Khan, M. E., & Zhuang, J., eds. (2012). *Diagnosing the Indonesian Economy: Toward Inclusive and Green Growth*. London: Anthem Press and Asian Development Bank.

Huff, T. (2011). *Intellectual Curiosity and the Scientific Revolution: A Global Perspective*. New York: Cambridge University Press.

Huff, T. (2017). *The Rise of Early Modern Science: Islam, China, and the West*, 3rd ed. New York: Cambridge University Press.

Hussein, A. A., Albar, M. A., & Alsanad, S. M. (2019). Prophetic medicine, Islamic medicine, traditional Arabic and Islamic medicine (TAIM): revisiting concepts and definitions. *Acta Scientific Medical Sciences*, 3(8), 62–69.

İhsanoğlu, E. M. (2004). *Science, Technology, and Learning in the Ottoman Empire: Western Influence, Local Institutions, and the Transfer of Knowledge*. Burlington: Ashgate/Variorum.

Iqtidar, H. (2011). *Secularizing Islamists? Jama 'at-e-Islami and Jama 'at-ud-Da 'wa in Urban Pakistan*. Chicago: University of Chicago Press.

Jaafar, A. N., & Wahiddin, M. R. (2016). A new quantum theory in accordance with Islamic science. In M. H. Kamali, O. Bakar, D. A. Batchelor & R. Hashim, eds., *Islamic Perspectives on Science and Technology: Selected Conference Papers*. Singapore: Springer, pp. 237–58.

Jalajel, D. S. (2009). *Islam and Biological Evolution: Exploring Classical Sources and Methodologies*. Western Cape: University of the Western Cape.

Janos, D. (2012). Qur'ānic cosmography in its historical perspective: Some notes on the formation of a religious worldview. *Religion*, 42(2), 215–31.

Kalın, İ. (2001). The sacred versus the secular: Nasr on science. In L. E. Hahn, R. E. Auxier, & L. W. Stone, eds., *Library of Living Philosophers: Seyyed Hossein Nasr*. Chicago: Open Court Press, pp. 445–62.

Kalın, İ. (2002). Three views of science in the Islamic world. In T. Peters, M. Iqbal, & S. N. Haq, eds., *God, Life, and the Cosmos: Christian and Islamic Perspectives*. New York: Routledge, pp. 43–75.

Kalın, İ. (2018). *Barbar, Modern, Medenî: Medeniyet Üzerine Notlar*. İstanbul: İnsan Yayınları.

Kaminski, J. J. (2021). *Islam, Liberalism, and Ontology: A Critical Re-evaluation*. New York: Routledge.

Karaömerlioğlu, M. A., & Yolun, M. (2020). Turkish nationalism and the evolutionary idea (1923–1938). *Nations and Nationalism*, 26, 743–58.

Kaya, V. (2012). Can the Quran support Darwin? an evolutionist approach by two Turkish scholars after the foundation of the Turkish Republic. *The Muslim World*, 102, 357–70.

Kaynar, M., & Parlak, İ. (2005). *Her İle Bir Üniversite: Türkiye'de Yüksek Öğretim Sisteminin Çöküşü*. Ankara: Paragraf Yayınevi.

Kazemipur, A. (2022). *Sacred as Secular: Secularization Under Theocracy in Iran*. Montreal: McGill-Queen's University Press.

Keener, C. S. (2011). *Miracles: The Credibility of the New Testament Accounts*. Grand Rapids: Baker Academic.

Keskin, T., ed. (2011). *The Sociology of Islam: Secularism, Economy and Politics*. Reading: Ithaca Press.

Kidd, I. J., José Medina, J., & Pohlhaus, Jr., G. (2017). *The Routledge Handbook of Epistemic Injustice*. New York: Routledge.

Kollu, H. Y., & Han, A. (2022). *Bilimin Anlatılmayan Tarihi*. Ankara: Lopus Yayınevi.

Koşar, U. (2013). *Allah De Ötesini Bırak*. İstanbul: Destek Yayınları.

Kuran, T. (2004). *Islam and Mammon: The Economic Predicaments of Islamism*. Princeton: Princeton University Press.

Kuran, T. (2011). *The Long Divergence: How Islamic Law Held Back the Middle East*. Princeton: Princeton University Press.

Kuru, A. T., & Stepan, A., eds. (2012). *Democracy, Islam, & Secularism in Turkey*. New York: Columbia University Press.

Kuru, A. T. (2019). *Islam, Authoritarianism, and Underdevelopment*. New York: Cambridge University Press.

Lachapelle, S. (2011). *Investigating the Supernatural: From Spiritism and Occultism to Psychical Research and Metapsychics in France, 1853–1931*. Baltimore: Johns Hopkins University Press.

Landau, J. M. (1974). *Radical Politics in Modern Turkey*. Leiden: Brill.

Langermann, Y. T., ed. (2012). *Monotheism & Ethics: Historical and Contemporary Intersections Among Judaism, Christianity, and Islam*. Leiden: Brill.

LeDrew, S. (2016). *The Evolution of Atheism: The Politics of a Modern Movement*. New York: Oxford University Press.

Livingston, J. W. (2018a). *The Rise of Science in Islam and the West: From Shared Heritage to Parting of The Ways, 8th to 19th Centuries*. New York: Routledge.

Livingston, J. W. (2018b). *In the Shadows of Glories Past: Jihad for Modern Science in Muslim Societies, 1850 to the Arab Spring*. New York: Routledge.

Ludwig, D., Koskinen, I., Mncube, Z., Poliseli, L., & Reyes-Galindo, L., eds. (2022). *Global Epistemologies and Philosophies of Science*. New York: Routledge.

Lumbard, J., & Nayed, A. A., eds. (2010). *The 500 Most Influential Muslims 2010*. Amman: Royal Islamic Strategic Studies Centre.

Madani, R. A. (2016). Islamization of science. *International Journal of Islamic Thought*, 9, 51–63.

Mahmood, S. (2001). Feminist theory, embodiment, and the docile agent: Some reflections on the Egyptian Islamic revival. *Cultural Anthropology* 16(2), 202–36.

Malik, S. A. (2018). *Atheism and Islam: A Contemporary Discourse*. Abu Dhabi: Kalam Research & Media.

Malik, S. A. (2019). Old texts, new masks: A critical review of misreading evolution onto historical Islamic texts. *Zygon*, 54, 501–22.

Malik, S. A. (2021). *Islam and Evolution: Al-Ghazālī and the Modern Evolutionary Paradigm*. New York: Routledge.

Malik, S. A., Karamali, H., & Khalayleh, M. Y. A. (2022). Does criticizing intelligent design (ID) undermine design discourse in the Qur'ān? a kalāmic response. *Zygon*, 57, 490–513.

Mansour, N. (2011). Science teachers' views of science and religion vs. the Islamic perspective: Conflicting or compatible? *Science Education*, 95(2), 281–309.

Mardin, Ş. (1989). *Religion and Social Change in Modern Turkey: The Case of Bediuzzaman Said Nursi*. Albany: State University of New York Press.

Markham, I. S., & Sayılgan, Z. (2017). *The Companion to Said Nursi Studies*. Eugene: Pickwick Publications.

Marks, J. (2013). *Ethics Without Morals: In Defense of Amorality*. New York: Routledge.

Masud, M. K. (2009). Islamic modernism. In M. K. Masud, A. Salvatore, & M. van Bruinessen, eds., *Islam and Modernity: Key Issues and Debates*. Edinburgh: Edinburgh University Press, pp. 237–60.

McCaffree, K. (2017). *The Secular Landscape: The Decline of Religion in America*. New York: Palgrave Macmillan.

McIntyre, L. (2019). *The Scientific Attitude: Defending Science from Denial, Fraud, and Pseudoscience.* Cambridge: The MIT Press.

Mirowski, P. (2011). *Science-Mart: Privatizing American Science.* Cambridge: Harvard University Press.

Mydin, L., Askari, H., & Mirakhor, A. (2018). *Resource Rich Muslim Countries and Islamic Institutional Reforms.* Pieterlen: Peter Lang.

Naguib, S. (2019). The hermeneutics of miracle: Evolution, eloquence, and the critique of scientific exegesis in the literary school of tafsīr. Part I: From Muḥammad ʿAbduh to Amīn al-Khūlī. *Journal of Qur'anic Studies.* 21(3), 57–88.

Nanda, M. (2003). *Prophets Facing Backward: Postmodern Critiques of Science and Hindu Nationalism in India.* Piscataway: Rutgers University Press.

Nanda, M. (2016). *Science in Saffron: Skeptical Essays on History of Science.* Palam Vihar: Three Essays Collective.

Nasr, S. H. (1987). *Knowledge and the Sacred.* Albany: State University of New York Press.

Nurbaki, H. (2022). *Kur'an-ı Kerim'den Ayetler ve İlmi Gerçekler.* 15th printing, Ankara: Türkiye Diyanet Vakfı.

Olson, R. G. (2008). *Science and Scientism in Nineteenth-century Europe.* Urbana: University of Illinois Press.

Oppenheim, J. (1985). *The Other World: Spiritualism and Psychical Research in England, 1850–1914.* New York: Cambridge University Press.

Orayj, K. (2022). Prophetic medicine: building an epistemological framework to overcome the conflict between religion and evidence-based medicine. *European Journal of Medicine and Natural Sciences,* 5(1), 44–62.

Ozan, E. D. (2012). *Gülme Sırası Bizde: 12 Eylül'e Giderken Sermaye Sınıfı Kriz ve Devlet.* İstanbul: Metis Yayınları.

Özgür, İ. (2012). *Islamic Schools in Modern Turkey: Faith, Politics, and Education.* New York: Cambridge University Press.

Parla, T., & Davison, A. (2004). *Corporatist Ideology in Kemalist Turkey.* New York: Syracuse University Press.

Peker, D., & Taşkın O. (2018). The enlightenment tradition and science education in Turkey. In M. R. Matthews, ed., *History, Philosophy, and Science Teaching.* Cham: Springer, pp. 67–97.

Peker, E. (2020). Beyond positivism: Building Turkish laiklik in the transition from the empire to the republic (1908–38). *Social Science History,* 44(2), 301–27.

Ramadan, T. (2009). *Radical Reform: Islamic Ethics and Liberation.* New York: Oxford University Press.

Rassool, G. H. (2019). *Evil Eye, Jinn Possession, and Mental Health Issues: An Islamic Perspective*. New York: Routledge.

Raudvere, C., & Stenberg, L., eds. (2009). *Sufism Today: Heritage and Tradition in the Global Community*. London: I. B. Tauris.

Reber, A. S., & Alcock, J. E. (2020). Searching for the impossible: Parapsychology's elusive quest. *American Psychologist*, 75(3), 391–99.

Riexinger, M. (2009). Responses of South Asian Muslims to the theory of evolution. *Welt des Islams*, 49(2), 212–47.

Riexinger, M. (2011). Islamic opposition to the Darwinian theory of evolution. In J. R. Lewis, & O. Hammer, eds., *Handbook of Religion and the Authority of Science*. Leiden: Brill, pp. 483–510.

Rizvi, A. A. (2016). *The Atheist Muslim: A Journey from Religion to Reason*. New York: St. Martin's Press.

Rosen, L. (2002). *The Culture of Islam: Changing Aspects of Contemporary Muslim Life*. Chicago: University of Chicago Press.

Russell, R. J. (2009). Divine action and quantum mechanics: a fresh assessment. In F. L. Shults, N. Murphy, & R. J. Russell, eds., *Philosophy, Science and Divine Action*. Boston: Brill, pp. 351–403.

Saif, L., Leoni, F., Melvin-Koushki, M., & Yahya, F., eds. (2021). *Islamicate Occult Sciences in Theory and Practice*. Leiden: Brill.

Salem, P. (1996). The rise and fall of secularism in the Arab world. *Middle East Policy*, 4, 147–60.

Saniotis, A. (2012). Muslims and ecology: fostering Islamic environmental ethics. *Contemporary Islam*, 6, 155–71.

Sardar, Z., ed. (1984). *The Touch of Midas: Science, Values, and Environment in Islam and the West*. Manchester: Manchester University Press.

Sardar, Z. (2006). *How Do You Know? Reading Ziauddin Sardar on Islam, Science and Cultural Relations*. London: Pluto Press.

Sardar, Z. (2011). *Reading the Qur'an: The Contemporary Relevance of the Sacred Text of Islam*. New York: Oxford University Press.

Sassower, R. (2015). *Compromising the Ideals of Science*. New York: Palgrave Macmillan.

Sax, W. S. (2020). The birth of the (exorcism) clinic: Media, modernity, and the jinn. In A. Michaels, & C. Wulf, eds., *Science and Scientification in South Asia and Europe*. London: Routledge, pp. 69–77.

Sayın, Ü., & Kence, A. (1999). Islamic scientific creationism. *Reports of the National Center for Science Education*, 19(6), 18–20, 25–29.

Sayksa, D. S., & Arni, J. (2016). Evidences of scientific miracle of Al-Qur'an in the modern era. *Jurnal Ushuluddin*, 24(1), 79–90.

Schielke, S. (2013). The Islamic world. In S. Bullivant and M. Ruse, eds., *The Oxford Handbook of Atheism*. Oxford: Oxford University Press.

Schnabel, L., & Bock, S. (2018). The persistent and exceptional intensity of American religion: A response to recent research. *Sociological Science*, 5, 711–21.

Scott, C. (2011). Science for the West, myth for the rest? The case of James Bay Cree knowledge construction. In S. Harding, ed., *The Postcolonial Science and Technology Studies Reader*. Durham: Duke University Press, pp. 175–97.

Setia, A. (2007). Three meanings of Islamic science: toward operationalizing Islamization of science. *Islam & Science*, 5(1), 23–52.

Şimşek, B., Aksoy, D. Y., Başaran, N. C. et al. (2017). Mapping traditional and complementary medicine in Turkey. *European Journal of Integrative Medicine*, 15, 68–72.

Sing, M. (2018). The tempestuous affair between Marxism and Islam: attraction, hostility, and accommodation since 1917. In B. Hendrich, ed., *Muslims and Capitalism: An Uneasy Relationship?* Baden-Baden: Ergon-Verlag, pp. 49–102.

Solberg, A. R. (2013). *The Mahdi Wears Armani: An Analysis of the Harun Yahya Enterprise*. Huddinge: Södertörns Högskola.

Somel, S. A. (2001). *The Modernization of Public Education in the Ottoman Empire 1839–1908: Islamization, Autocracy and Discipline*. Leiden: Brill.

Soofi, A. S., & Ghazinoory, S. (2013). *Science and Innovations in Iran: Development, Progress, and Challenges*. New York: Palgrave Macmillan.

Soyubol, K. (2021). In search of perfection: Neo-spiritualism, Islamic mysticism, and secularism in Turkey. *Modern Intellectual History*, 18(1), 70–94.

Stiedenroth, K. S. (2020). *Unani Medicine in the Making: Practices and Representations in 21st-century India*. Amsterdam: Amsterdam University Press.

Tarhan, N. (2021). *İnanç Psikolojisi ve Bilim: Ruh, Beyin ve Akıl Üçgeninde İnsanoğlu*. 17th printing, İstanbul: Timaş Yayınları.

Tart, C. T. (2009). *The End of Materialism: How Evidence of the Paranormal Is Bringing Science and Spirit Together*. Oakland: New Harbinger.

Taslaman, C. (2007). *Evrim Teorisi, Felsefe ve Tanrı*. İstanbul: İstanbul Yayınevi.

Taslaman, C. (2008). *Kuantum Teorisi, Felsefe ve Tanrı*. İstanbul: İstanbul Yayınevi.

Tee, C. (2016). *The Gülen Movement in Turkey: The Politics of Islam and Modernity*. London: I. B. Tauris.

Tegmark, M. (2014). *Our Mathematical Universe: My Quest for the Ultimate Nature of Reality.* New York: Alfred E. Knopf.

Tekerek, T. (2023). *Taşra Üniversiteleri: AK Partinin Arka Kampüsü.* İstanbul: İletişim Yayınları.

Telliel, Y. D. (2019). Miraculous evidence: scientific wonders and religious reasons. *Comparative Studies of South Asia, Africa and the Middle East,* 39(3), 528–42.

Toosi, J. F. (2019). A model for reconciling Islamic teachings with the intellectual and scientific achievements of modernity. *Islam and Civilisational Renewal Journal,* 10(2), 264–79.

Tuğal, C. (2009). *Passive Revolution: Absorbing the Islamic Challenge to Capitalism.* Stanford: Stanford University Press.

Turner, J. H., Maryanski, A., Petersen, A. K., & Geertz, A. W., eds. (2017). *The Emergence and Evolution of Religion: By Means of Natural Selection.* Milton Park: Taylor & Francis.

Vaditya, V. (2018). Social domination and epistemic marginalisation: Towards methodology of the oppressed. *Social Epistemology,* 32(4), 272–85.

van Bruinessen, M. (2009). Sufism, "popular" Islam and the encounter with modernity. In M. K. Masud, A. Salvatore, & M. van Bruinessen, eds., *Islam and Modernity: Key Issues and Debates.* Edinburgh: Edinburgh University Press, pp. 125–57.

Van Eyghen, H., & Szocik, K. (2021). *Revising Cognitive and Evolutionary Science of Religion: Religion as an Adaptation.* Cham: Springer Nature.

Varisco, D. (2018). Darwin and dunya: Muslim responses to Darwinian evolution. *Journal of International and Global Studies,* 9(2), 14–39.

Weller, P. (2022). *Fethullah Gülen's Teaching and Practice: Inheritance, Context, and Interactive Development.* Cham: Palgrave Macmillan.

Wilkins, J. (2013). Biological essentialism. In K. Kampourakis, ed., *The Philosophy of Biology: A Companion for Educators.* Dordrecht: Springer, pp. 395–419.

Williams, R. N., & Robinson, D. N., eds. (2015). *Scientism: The New Orthodoxy.* New York: Bloomsbury Academic.

Wright, J. E. (2000). *The Early History of Heaven.* New York: Oxford University Press.

Yahya, H. (1997). *Evrim Aldatmacası: Evrim Teorisi'nin Bilimsel Çöküşü ve Teorinin İdeolojik Arka Planı.* İstanbul: Vural Yayıncılık.

Yalçınoğlu, P. (2009). Impacts of anti-evolutionist movements on educational policies and practices in USA and Turkey. *İlköğretim Online,* 8(1), 254–67.

Yankaya, D. (2014). *Yeni İslâmî Burjuvazi: Türk Modeli.* İstanbul: İletişim Yayınları.

Yıldız, A., Korkmaz, N., & Doğan, N., eds. (2019). *Tarihten Güncele Laik Eğitim: Kavramlar, Deneyimler, Sorunlar.* İstanbul: Kalkedon Yayıncılık.

Yudell, M. (2014). *Race Unmasked: Biology and Race in the Twentieth Century.* New York: Columbia University Press.

Ziadat, A. A. (1986). *Western Science in the Arab World: The Impact of Darwinism 1860–1930.* New York: Palgrave Macmillan.

Cambridge Elements

Islam and the Sciences

Nidhal Guessoum
American University of Sharjah, United Arab Emirates
Nidhal Guessoum is Professor of Astrophysics at the American University of Sharjah, United Arab Emirates. Besides Astrophysics, he has made notable contributions in Science & Islam/ Religion, education, and the public understanding of science; he has published books on these subjects in several languages, including *The Story of the Universe* (in Arabic, first edition in 1997), *Islam's Quantum Question* (in English in 2010, translated into several languages), and *The Young Muslim's Guide to Modern Science* (in English 2019, translated into several languages), numerous articles (academic and general-public), and vast social-media activity.

Stefano Bigliardi
Al Akhawayn University in Ifrane, Morocco
Stefano Bigliardi is Associate Professor of Philosophy at Al Akhawayn University in Ifrane, Morocco. He trained as a philosopher of science, has a PhD in philosophy from the University of Bologna; and has been serving in different positions at universities in Germany, Sweden, Mexico, and Switzerland. He has published a monograph and a general-public book on Islam and Science as well as dozens of articles (peer-reviewed and popular) on the subject and others. Since 2016, he has taught undergraduate courses on Islam and Science at Al Akhawayn University in Ifrane, Morocco.

About the Series
Elements in Islam and the Sciences is a new platform for the exploration, critical review and concise analysis of Islamic engagements with the sciences: past, present and future. The series will not only assess ideas, arguments and positions; it will also present novel views that push forward the frontiers of the field. These Elements will evince strong philosophical, theological, historical, and social dimensions as they address interactions between Islam and a wide range of scientific subjects.

Cambridge Elements $\equiv$

Islam and the Sciences

Elements in the Series

A full series listing is available at: www.cambridge.org/EISC

Printed in the United States
by Baker & Taylor Publisher Services